STARK

TRAINING Grundwissen ENGLISCH

Liam Cleary

Englisch 9. Klasse

Aufgaben mit Lösungen

STARK

Bildnachweis

S. 15: Reproduced by permission of Oxford University Press from Oxford Advanced Learner's Dictionary (5th edition) Oxford, © Oxford University Press 1995; S. 24: Van Morrison, Hymns To The Silence, © 1991 Polygram Music Publishing Ltd; The Cranberries: no need to argue, © 1994 Island Records Inc.; S. 32: Trude Fleischmann, New York; S. 38, 110, 133, 135, 142: Liam Cleary, Coburg; S. 58: The Christian Science Monitor, © 1990 The Christian Science Publishing Society; S. 70: Wendy O'Shea, Sunday Independent, Dublin, November 24, 1996; S. 72: Will Rogers Memorial and Birthplace Ranch of Oklahoma, USA; S. 84: Wendy O'Shea: O'Brian. Town House Publishers, Dublin 1985; S. 87: Scotland on Sunday, 4. 11. 1997; S. 102: The Hockey Hall of Fame, Toronto; S. 115: American Studies Newsletter 33, Mai 1994; S. 116: Archiv für Kunst und Geschichte, Berlin; S. 129: b) http://www.camelotintl.com/royal/charles.html; c) Transglobe; S. 137: American Studies Newsletter 34, September 1994; S. 138: c) American Studies Newsletter, Mai 1988; f) American Studies Newsletter 34, September 1994; S. 139: Wendy O'Shea: O'Brian. Town House Publishers, Dublin 1985; S. 141: Richard Wilson, Sunday Times 4. Mai 1997; S. 145: Wilson Hartnell, Dublin; S. 148: Photo taken by Caroline Forbes, Faber and Faber Publishers, London; S. 150: USIA

ISBN-13: 978-3-89449-322-6
ISBN-10: 3-89449-322-4

D-85318 Freising · Postfach 1852 · Tel. (08161) 1790

Inhalt

Fortsetzung siehe nächste Seite

Autor: Liam Cleary
Illustrator: Igor Schulz-Bertram

Vorwort

Liebe Schülerin, lieber Schüler,

du bist Schülerin oder Schüler der Mittelstufe des Gymnasiums und tust dich schwer in Englisch? Das vorliegende Buch hilft dir, den Englischstoff der 9. Klasse zu **verstehen** und anhand von zahlreichen **Aufgaben zu üben**.

- Jeder Abschnitt beginnt mit Erklärungen und Regeln, die in übersichtlicher und kompakter Weise das notwendige **Grundwissen** vermitteln. Daran schließen sich **Beispiele** an.
- Vielfältiges Aufgabenmaterial – häufig auch zur **Textproduktion** – ermöglicht **das individuelle Üben** des gelernten Stoffs. Die Aufgaben sind nach ihrem Schwierigkeitsgrad gestaffelt. Besonders schwere Übungen sind mit einem * markiert. Zu allen Aufgaben gibt es ausführliche **Lösungen**.
- Neben dem Unterricht kannst du dieses Buch zur **Wiederholung und Festigung** des Lehrstoffs einsetzen.
- Du kannst dich damit auch gezielt auf **Klassen- bzw. Schularbeiten** vorbereiten.
- Und du kannst es am Ende der 9. Klasse dazu verwenden, den gesamten Lehrstoff zu wiederholen, insbesondere dann, wenn du dich auf die **Nachprüfung** in Englisch für die 9. Klasse vorbereiten möchtest.

Ich wünsche dir viel Erfolg und Freude bei der Arbeit mit diesem Buch!

Mit besten Grüßen
dein „Trainer“

Liam Cleary

Liam Cleary

… rund ums Nomen

1 Präpositionen

Präpositionen *(prepositions)* sind **Verhältniswörter** wie beispielsweise *under, between, for.* Sie stehen meist vor einem Nomen oder einem Pronomen und haben die Aufgabe, das von ihnen abhängige Wort mit einem anderen zu verbinden und dadurch die Art des Verhältnisses zwischen dem in beiden Wörtern Genannten auszudrücken.

Wann verwendest du *prepositions?*

Du verwendest Präpositionen, wenn du

- ein **Verhältnis der Zeit**

  Beispiel: Peter came at 3 o'clock.
- ein **Verhältnis des Ortes** oder der **Richtung**

  Beispiel: The book is under the bed.
- oder ein **anderes Verhältnis**

  Beispiele: Eamonn worked with me for a while.
  She kept smoking despite what her doctor said.

Rund um die Präpositionen des Ortes und der Richtung

Es gibt nur **wenige Regeln** für die Verwendung von *prepositions.* Jedes Auftauchen einer *preposition* sollte als Einzelfall angesehen, im Wörterbuch nachgeschlagen und dann entsprechend **gelernt** werden. Folgende ***prepositions of place and direction*** und ihre Bedeutungen solltest du kennen:

prepositions		*Beispiele:*
about	herum	The children ran about to keep warm.
above	über	We could see an aeroplane above the town.
across	durch	He waded across a river.
	über	He ran across the road.

after	nach	Gorey was the next town after Arklow.
	nachdem	After he had eaten he went out.
against	gegen	The wardrobe was standing against the back wall.
among	unter	I saw Sara among the crowd.
	zwischen	The ball could be seen among the bushes.
around	um	Ted was ill around Christmas.
	herum	He ran around the room looking for a chair.
at	am	Ann was waiting for him at the airport.
	bei	Peter met his wife at a party.
	im	At the age of 16 Peter started smoking.
	zu	I bought many presents at Christmas.
before	bevor	The President stood before his people.
behind	hinter	We walked behind the hearse.
below	unter(halb von)	The sailors were below deck.
beside	neben	The police station is situated beside the school.
between	zwischen	The picture is between the poster and the painting.
by	an	She played 'Down by the Riverside'.
from	von	Jane walked from Land's End to John o'Groats.
in	in	He lives in Wales.
inside	innerhalb	We saw the doctor inside the prison camp.
into	in … hinein	We walked into the theatre.
near	in der Nähe von	I was sitting near the prime minister.
of	von	The man lived within a mile of the town.
off	von	He jumped off the boat.
on	auf	The brush lay on the table.
over	über	The cow jumped over the moon.
past	vorbei	She rushed past me.
through	durch	We walked through the forest.
towards	auf … zu	I ran towards my uncle.

Aufgabe 1 Put in the correct preposition from this list: *above, on, in, at, to, off, under, from, behind, beside, outside, through, on top of.*

a)

Every morning Tom stands _________ a queue _____________ the bus stop and waits for the schoolbus.

b) 

The captain looks ______________ the periscope to see what's _____________ the water.

c) 

After the ceremony friends of the newly-married couple drove ______________ them to the hotel.

d) 

When he won the pools he was ____________________ the world.

e) 

The bank is ____________ the Savoy Hotel _____________ Main Street.

Aufgabe 2 Put in the right prepositions.

To: Jenny Doyle
High St.
Wicklow

July 1, 2004

Dear Jenny,

Just a short note from Italy. We are ____ the seaside! There's a fat man lying ____ an airbed and loads of people are fishing ____ the pier. A few yards away children are digging a hole ___ the sand. I see an old woman putting a magazine ____ her handbag. My brother is testing out his new goggles and swimming ___ the water. There's a lifebuoy tied ___ the railings in case he gets __ trouble! There's the most beautiful sailing boat you ever saw ___ the horizon and I see a young dog running ___ the water. My girlfriend June is lying __ me __ her new bikini and there's a sunshade ___ her head. Another girl we know has just walked __, carrying her surfboard and pointing ___ the waves. Typical holiday bliss! And there's not a cloud ___ the sky!

See you soon.

Love,
Denise

Rund um die Präpositionen der Zeit

Auch folgende ***prepositions of time*** solltest du kennen und gegebenenfalls auswendig lernen:

prepositions		*Beispiele:*
after	nach	We went to the cinema after dinner.
at	um	The robber boarded the train at 6.15 a. m.
before	vor	The cars will not be repaired before Tuesday.
by	im	By the age of seven Ann had learned to play chess.
during	während	We got two postcards from Canada during that period.
for	für	Tom was in Canada for two weeks.
in	in	"I'll be with you in a minute!"
on	an	We arrived on Wednesday.
since	seit	She had been waiting since 3 o'clock.
until	bis	The doctor told Dave to stay in bed until Monday.
while	während	While the show was in progress he worked backstage.

Manche Präpositionen können auch **verschiedene Arten von Verhältnissen** beschreiben, **je nachdem, mit welchem Wort sie verknüpft sind**.

Beispiele:	Mary is in hospital.	(place)
	He arrived in time.	(time)
	Karl is in training.	(situation)

Aufgabe 3 Fill in the right prepositions from the following list: *until, before, after, during, at, while, for, in, since, by, from, on.*

a) I have to teach a class ______________ 3.15.

b) We will see you ______________ the New Year.

c) The cock crows ______________ dawn.

d) I have been living in Germany ______________ ten years.

e) The baby woke four times ______________ the night.

f) We will go to the park ______________ the news is over.

g) The doctor arrived just ______________ time to save the child.

h) If you don't stop smoking you will have a cough ______________ long.

i) If it hasn't stopped snowing ______________ three o'clock we will postpone the game.

j) Alan won't be here ______________ tomorrow morning.

k) The prisoners escaped ____________ the guards were watching TV.

l) ____________ the time they realized they were gone it was too late.

m) When ____________ last the prisoners were recaptured they had been 36 hours out of prison.

n) She eats fish ____________ Fridays.

o) Diarmaid was born ____________ the 18th of April.

p) I'll be back ____________ two hours.

q) There is nobody in the library ____________ the moment.

Rund um *since* und *for*

Das deutsche **,seit'** wird im Englischen mit ***for*** übersetzt, wenn es eine **Zeitspanne** beschreibt, mit ***since***, wenn es sich um einen **Zeitpunkt** handelt.

Beispiel: I have known Gerard for years, since 1957 in fact.

Beachte: *Since* und *for* werden oft im *present perfect progressive* benutzt.

Aufgabe 4 Jim is talking to Sue, an old friend in England, who is asking him for all his news. However, they need a bit of help. Can you build the parts into full sentences? In most cases you should use the *present perfect progressive.* Use *since* or *for* as appropriate.

SUE: How are you Jim?
JIM: Fine thanks Sue.
SUE: How long/you/to live in France now?

____

JIM: I/to live in France/1980 and in Paris itself/4 years.

____

SUE: How's your French, Jim?
JIM: Quite good. I/to learn French/a long time.

____

SUE: What have you been doing in your spare time lately?
JIM: Well I/to attend a first aid course/Christmas and I/to learn to dance/the past six months.

____

SUE: You/see/any good plays/lately?

____

JIM: No. I/not/to attend the theatre/this year.

____

SUE: How long have you been working as a teacher Jim?

JIM: I/to work in my present school/1994 and before that I taught in Lyons for a while.

____

SUE: Would you not like to return to England?

JIM: Oh yes, I/to try/to get a job in England/ages.

____

Aufgabe 5 Look at the picture and describe what you see.

a)

The building is _on_ _fire_.

b)

The workers are ______________ ______________.

c)

The workers are gone ______________ ______________.

d)

He is paying for the bike ______________ ______________.

e) 

She is paying ____________ ____________.

f) 

He is ____________ ____________ with her.

Rund um die Präpositionen nach bestimmten Ausdrücken

Manche Wörter sind im Englischen fest mit einer bestimmten Präposition verbunden. Lerne diese Wörter mit ihren Präpositionen auswendig!

to laugh at	lachen über
to deal with	etwas behandeln
to dream of	träumen von
to feel sorry for	Leid tun
to be good at	gut sein in
to depart for	abfahren
to arrive at	ankommen
to learn from	ersehen aus
to get angry at	ärgerlich werden über
to get interested in	sich interessieren für
to apologize for	sich entschuldigen für
to be careless about	gleichgültig sein gegen

Aufgabe 6 Complete these sentences with the correct phrase from the list.

Dr. Callaghan is talking about himself to a fellow doctor.

When I was small I (1) *dreamt of* becoming a doctor. But it was at university that I really (2) ____________ medicine. I'm married to a girl from my own home town and I (3) ____________ work at 7.00 a. m. every day. Usually I (4) ____________ the office at 7.45. I have been working in neurology for many years and I (5) ____________ patients who suffer from serious brain disorders. I get frustrated with patients who are (6) ____________ taking their medicine. I (7) ______________ them all and do my best to help them. I (8) ___________ stupid, mean people who (9) ___________ my patients or the illnesses they have. People say I'm (10) _____________ my work which is a nice compliment but I always try and (11) _____________ any error I make. Years ago my father told me "always (12) _____________ your mistakes" and that was good advice.

Manche Wörter verändern im Englischen ihre Bedeutung, je nachdem, welche Präposition sie nach sich ziehen. Lerne auch sie auswendig!

to look for	*to look after*	*to blow up*	*to blow out*
to cut off	*to cut down*	*to get on to*	*to get off*
to give out	*to give away*	*to pick out*	*to pick up*
to put out	*to put on*	*to turn down*	*to turn into*

Aufgabe 7 Write the correct phrase from the above list under the pictures.

to get on to

____

____

____

____

____

WANTED!
WANTED!
WANTED!

CHURCH HILL
4

Aufgabe 8*

Mixed exercise: Fill in the prepositions and write a story in English.

Matt O'Brien and Lucy Hartmann were dancing the fox trot (1) _on_ ______ the wooden floor of the Rialto ballroom. Matt, a tramworker, and Lucy, a worker (2) ______ Crawford's biscuit factory, had only recently started keeping company. It was (3) ______ such a Rialto tea dance one Saturday afternoon that they had met. When, near the interval, Jack McCormack and his band played a version of "The Leaving of Liverpool" Matt's thoughts seemed to wander. "Thinking of Nelly are you?" Lucy whispered. Matt's sister Nelly was due to leave (4) ______ America (5) ______ a White Star Liner the following evening. It made him sad to think he might never see her again though he knew it was what she had always wanted. Once the song was over, Matt went to get Lucy's coat. This evening they would go home early to spend a last few hours (6) ______ Nelly.

It was on the way (7) ______ the ballroom that the trouble started. The Dobson twins, or 'ruffians' as Matt's mother called them, were standing near the door. Harry Dobson caught hold (8) ______ Lucy's arm and said "Lucy, stay (9) ______ one more dance". "Hands off!", cried Lucy. "She doesn't like you Harry", laughed Mikey Dobson, who had placed himself between Matt and Lucy. Harry Dobson gripped Lucy's arm tighter and said "Now luv, don't be a spoilsport. Just one dance." "Keep your filthy paws (10) ______ yourself Dobson", he shouted, and burst (11) ______ Mikey to stand (12) ______ Harry Dobson and Lucy. "Who asked you", sneered Dobson, grabbing Matt (13) ______ the throat. His clenched fist struck Matt (14) ______ the jaw. Matt hit back. Lucy screamed. Afterwards neither of them could remember which (15) ______ the Dobsons had pulled the knife. All they knew was that somehow Matt had got hold of it. Matt said he would never be able to forget the terrible look on Harry Dobson's face.

Nelly O'Brien was sitting (16) ______ her parents (17) ______ the kitchen table when the door burst open and Lucy, completely out-of-breath, came in with Matt a few steps (18) ______ her. His mouth was bleeding and he looked shocking. He had lost his cap somewhere in Upper Parliament Street. It didn't take long to relate what had happened. "Do you think Dobson's dead" his father asked? I'm not sure, I just don't know. "You'll have to go (19) ______ the police", said his mother. "You won't stand a chance", his father shouted. "The Dobsons have friends (20) ______ high places." (21) ______ a moment there was silence. "Is this really happening", sobbed Lucy. "It was self-defence, Matt, self-defence", she continued. "Son, you've never broken the law before," his mother said. "But Ma, Dobson may be dead. I'll be given ten years, maybe more." Suddenly Nelly O'Brien spoke up. "I've been thinking, Matt. Why don't you take my ticket? There's no name (22) ______________ it. They'll never trace you in the States." "But Nelly you have been dreaming (23) ______________ this (24) ______________ years. You always wanted to go there. I can't…" Suddenly the sound of footsteps at the top (25) ______________ the street made up his mind (26) ______________ him. "The police" shouted Lucy who was standing (27) ______________ the window of the tenement house. Following his sister and Lucy (28) ______________ his bedroom Matt put Nelly's ticket, his passport and some belongings (29) ______________ a suitcase. Seconds later someone was knocking (30) ______________ the front door. "Matt, you'll be needing this." Nelly shoved all her savings, six pounds ten shillings, (31) ______________ his jacket pocket. After opening the bedroom window Matt turned, kissed the girls and climbed out into the starless December night. Minutes later, with the police interviewing his parents as to his whereabouts, Matt was making his way (32) ______________ the backstreets and alleyways of the Liverpool of his childhood. The next his family would hear (33) ______________ him would be in a letter addressed 105 Washington Square, Syracuse, New York.

Aufgabe 9 **Mixed exercise:** Put in the missing prepositions.

a) Deirdre and I got engaged ____________ 1.30 ____________ Thursday the 19th ____________ April.

b) Did the first London folk festival take place ____________ 1969?

c) It rained cats and dogs ____________ nearly the entire festival.

d) ____________ the end of the festival most people were drenched.

e) ____________ the time you read this letter I will be ____________ London.

f) Lenny dropped ____________ last night.

g) She wasn't a bit surprised ____________ his behaviour.

h) My father always boils potatoes ____________ their jackets.

i) A knowledge ____________ languages is a good thing.

j) The referee wrote __________ the player's name in his book.

k) We have been learning Dutch __________ 3 years now.

l) The shop is open __________ 5 p.m.

m) For days __________ the flood, the roads were covered __________ water.

n) Dora is interested __________ farming.

o) French was too hard __________ me.

p) We put the cat __________ the door.

q) Andy is often mistaken __________ his twin brother.

r) There has been an increase __________ unemployment.

s) The child did damage __________ the TV.

t) Harry has a good attitude __________ his work.

u) His writing was rejected __________ many editors.

v) Do you expect a rise __________ salary this year!

w) Are you aware __________ Tom's drink problem?

x) I'm hopeless __________ chess.

y) Séan is engaged __________ Moira.

z) Can you give me £ 10? I'm short __________ money.

Aufgabe 10*

Creative Writing

You receive an e-mail from a good friend with a photo of the new school he is attending. Write back describing your reaction to his e-mail and tell him how things are in your school. Use as many prepositions as possible.

2 Adjektive

Adjektive (*adjectives*) sind Wörter wie *small, several, yellow, nice*. Mit ihnen kann man die **Eigenschaften** oder **Merkmale von Lebewesen, Dingen, Begriffen, Zuständen, Vorgängen** und **Tätigkeiten näher beschreiben**.

2.1 Einsatzmöglichkeiten von Adjektiven

An welche Stelle im Satz stellst du das Adjektiv?

- Das Adjektiv steht fast immer **vor dem Nomen**, zu dem es gehört (= attributiver Gebrauch).

  Beispiel: The girl in the red dress went into the small cottage.

- Manchmal kann das Adjektiv auch **nach dem Nomen**, zu dem es gehört, stehen.

  Beispiel: The night, dark and starless, was a bad one to be out in the cold.

- Wird **mehr als ein Adjektiv** gebraucht, um ein Nomen zu charakterisieren, ist die **Reihenfolge wichtig:** Adjektive, die eine Meinung ausdrücken, werden in der Regel vor Adjektive gestellt, die einen Fakt beschreiben. Gleiches gilt für Adjektive der Größe und Länge. Sie stehen meist vor solchen Adjektiven, die die Form und Breite von Objekten beschreiben.

  Beispiele: Kevin lives in a nice, semi-detached house in Cranbrooke.
  Susan swims in a big, round pool every day.
  There is a long, narrow driveway in front of the house.

- Das Adjektiv kann aber auch **nach bestimmten Verben** – vor allem nach *be* – stehen (= prädikativer Gebrauch).

  Beispiel: *The girl is strong.*

Aufgabe 1 **Vocabulary:** Before you begin this chapter of exercises read the following:

In einigen Übungen dieses Buches sollst du trainieren, wie man mit einem einsprachigen Wörterbuch umgeht. Hier ein paar Tipps dazu:

- Bevor du mit der Suche nach Wörtern in deinem Wörterbuch beginnst, solltest du dir das Verzeichnis mit den in deinem Wörterbuch benutzten **Abkürzungen** genau anschauen.
- Wenn du ein Wort nachschlägst, solltest du erst **alle Bedeutungsvarianten durchgehen**, die in deinem Wörterbuch verzeichnet sind. Erst wenn du alle gelesen hast, solltest du dich für eine Bedeutung entscheiden.

- In einem Wörterbuch zu lesen, ist eine gute Methode, eine Fremdsprache kennen zu lernen. Das folgende Beispiel soll dir dies erläutern: Angenommen, du liest einen Text, in dem das englische Wort counter vorkommt. Wir nehmen weiter an, dass dir dieses Wort unbekannt ist. Du schlägst also in deinem Wörterbuch nach und findest diesen oder einen ähnlichen Eintrag:

coun·ter[1] /'kaunta(r)/ *n* a long flat surface over which goods are sold or business is done in a shop, bank, etc: *chocolate displayed on the counter* ◦ *the ticket reservation counter.* IDM **over the 'counter 1** (of medicines) that can be bought without a PRESCRIPTION(1a): *These tablets are available over the counter.* **2** without a special licence or arrangement: *buying guns over the counter.* **under the 'counter** (of goods bought or sold) secretly and sometimes illegally: *Pornography is no longer sold under the counter in many countries.*

coun·ter[2] /'kaunta(r)/ *n* **1** a small disc used for playing or scoring in certain board games. **2** (esp in compounds) an electronic device for counting sth: *an engine's rev counter* ◦ *You need to reset the counter.* See also BARGAINING COUNTER.

coun·ter[3] /'kaunta(r)/ *adv* ~ **to sth** in the opposite direction to sth; in opposition to sth: *act counter to one's wishes* ◦ *Economic trends are* ***running counter to*** *the forecasts.*

coun·ter[4] /'kaunta(r)/ *v* ~ **(with sth)**; ~ **sb/sth (with sth)** to respond to sb/sth with an opposing view, an attack, etc: [Vpr] *Linda countered with a joke of her own.* [V.speech] *'A Scotsman might not agree with that,' she countered.* [Vn] *Such arguments are easily countered.* [Vnpr] *The senator countered his critics with a strong speech defending his policies.* [V.that] *I pointed out the shortcomings of the scheme, but he countered that the plans were not yet finished.*

In der ersten Erklärung kannst du erfahren, dass ein *counter* einem „Ladentisch“, einem „Schalter“ oder einer „Theke“ entspricht. Wenn du jetzt weiterliest, siehst du, dass *to buy sth. 'over the counter'* „etwas kaufen“ bedeutet, während *to buy sth. 'under the counter'* „etwas unter der Hand, heimlich oder illegal erwerben“ heißt. Der Auschnitt oben zeigt dir, dass es aber noch viele andere Bedeutungsvarianten des Wortes gibt.

- Das einsprachige Wörterbuch sagt dir nicht nur, was ein bestimmtes Wort bedeutet, du kannst auch erfahren, wie die einzelnen Wörter ausgesprochen werden.

Und nun kannst du sicherlich die Bedeutung der folgenden Wörter aus deinem Wörterbuch erschließen:

counterpart a person or thing which corresponds to or has the same function as s.b./sth.

cute ______

tedious ______

evil ______

rating ______

stunt ______

superficial ______

Aufgabe 2 Write the adjectives given in the picture in the right order.

nice, young

a nice young girl

blue-eyed, cute

middle-aged, angry

ugly, tattered

dark-haired, gorgeous

black, horrid

filthy, grey

Irish, beautiful, well-known

tedious, first, badly-written

expensive, unattractive

Wird ein Artikel vorangestellt, kann das Adjektiv als Nomen gebraucht werden. **Nominal gebrauchte Adjektive beschreiben eine Gruppe** von Menschen. Sie werden wie Pluralformen verwendet, haben aber kein Plural-s. Wenn einzelne Personen gemeint sind, so musst du das Adjektiv durch ein Nomen ergänzen, was dann wieder dem attributiven Gebrauch entspricht.

Bespiele: The poor suffer greatly in winter.
The old woman is often very lonely at Christmas.

Aufgabe 3 Translation.

a) Ist dein Englischlehrer Engländer oder Amerikaner?

b) Die Reichen bleiben oft unter sich.

c) Für Blinde ist das Leben ohne Hilfe schwer.

d) Die Franzosen singen und tanzen gern.

e) Im Tierreich fressen die Starken die Schwachen.

f) Die Jungen sind oft ungeduldig mit den Alten.

g) Die Holländer sind eine Weltmacht im Fußball.

h) Taube können in bestimmten Schulen lernen, sich zu verständigen.

i) Das Gute im Menschen wird oft nicht erkannt.

j) Man kümmert sich oft nicht genügend um Behinderte.

k) Die Indianer ehrten ihre Toten in Geschichten und Gesängen.

Aufgabe 4* **Tricky word families:** For this exercise you are allowed to use a dictionary. Study these verbs and complete the word family by writing in their adjective and noun. In some cases more than one answer is possible. If you don't understand the verb check its meaning in the dictionary and write the German in the space provided.

Verb	German meaning	Adjective	Noun
to adapt	anpassen	adaptable	the adaptation
to admit			
to allow			
to avoid			
to believe			
to blind			
to depart			
to describe			
to die			
to demand			
to enjoy			
to escape			
to free			
to harm			
to include			
to persuade			
to revolt			
to sell			
to succeed			
to surprise			
to taste			
to understand			

Es gibt einige **Adjektive**, die auf ***-ing* oder *-ed*** enden könnnen. Sie sehen sich sehr ähnlich, haben aber eine **unterschiedliche Bedeutung**. Daher darfst du sie nicht verwechseln.

Bespiele: Dave is interested in history.
Dave ist an Geschichte interessiert.

Dave finds history very interesting.
Dave findet Geschichte sehr interessant.

Aufgabe 5 Take the following pairs and put them in the right places under the pictures: *tired/tiring, exciting/excited, terrifying/terrified, depressed/depressing, confusing/confused, amazing/amazed, boring/bored.*

a)

Jane is ____________________ because the game is ____________________.

b)

Tony was ____________________ by the ____________________ sight of a ghost.

c)

The crowd were __________________ by the acrobat's __________________ stunts.

d)

Mr McFly got very __________________ doing the __________________ weightlifting exercises.

e)

John got very ______________ when he heard the ______________ news.

f)

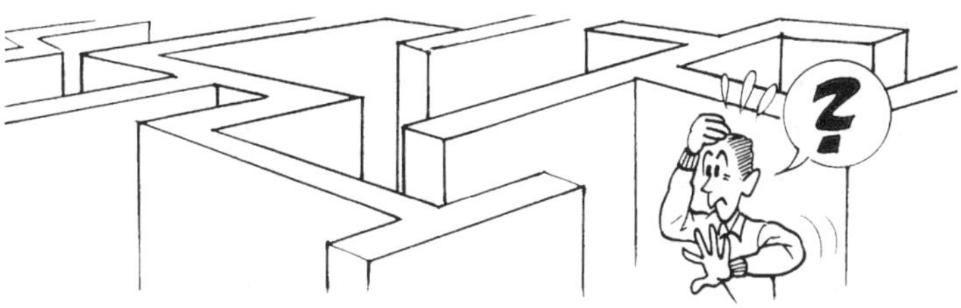

Because the maze is very ______________, Tom is ______________.

g)

Jack gets very __________ at work because his job is ______________.

2.2 Adjektive – Steigerung und Vergleiche

Wann steigerst du Adjektive?

Steigerungsformen verwendest du dann, wenn du verschiedene **Abstufungen von Eigenschaften** ausdrücken willst.

Beispiel:	My painting is nice.	(Positiv)
	Jon's painting is nicer.	(Komparativ)
	Anne's is the nicest.	(Superlativ)

Wann verwendest du Vergleiche?

Du gebrauchst **Vergleiche**, wenn du **Gleichheit** oder **Ungleichheit** beschreiben willst.

Beispiel: My bike is faster than yours.

Wie bildest du die Steigerungsformen der Adjektive?

- **Einsilbige Adjektive** und **zweisilbige** Adjektive auf *-le*, *-er*, *-y* und *-ow* werden gesteigert, indem du an die Grundform *-er* oder *-est* anhängst.
  Beispiel: narrow → narrower → narrowest
- Nach einem **kurzen einfachen Vokal** musst du den Endkonsonanten verdoppeln und *-er* oder *-est* anhängen.
  Beispiel: big → bigger → biggest
- Endet das **Adjektiv auf *-e***, hängst du nur *-r* oder *-st* an.
  Beispiel: large → larger → largest
- Bei **zweisilbigen Adjektiven auf *-y*** wird bei der Steigerung das *-y* zu *-i*.
  Beispiel: friendly → friendlier → friendliest
- **Zweisilbige Adjektive**, die nicht auf *-le*, *-er*, *-y* und *-ow* enden sowie **mehrsilbige Adjektive** steigerst du, indem du dem Adjektiv *more* oder *most* voranstellst.
  Beispiel: beautiful → more beautiful → most beautiful
- Einige Adjektive haben **unregelmäßige Steigerungsformen**. Diese musst du auswendig lernen!

Beispiele:	good	→	better	→	best
	bad	→	worse	→	worst
	little	→	less	→	least
	much/many	→	more	→	most
	far	→	further	→	furthest
	ill	→	worse	→	worst

Wie bildest du Vergleiche?

- **Unterschiedliche Dinge** vergleichst du, indem du den Komparativ des Adjektivs mit *than* gebrauchst.
  Beispiel: My bike is more expensive than yours.
- Die **Gleichheit zweier Dinge** wird mit *as* + Positiv des Adjektivs + *as* ausgedrückt.
  Beispiel: My bike is as expensive as yours.
- Die **Ungleichheit zweier Dinge** musst du durch *not* + as + Positiv des Adjektivs + *as* ausdrücken.
  Beispiel: My bike is not as expensive as yours.

Aufgabe 6 Work with a partner! Choose a list each, call out the adjectives and ask your partner to give and spell the comparative and superlative forms of the adjectives. One point for every correct answer.

List A	List B
dark	fast
brainy	dreamy
impossible	severe
wonderful	hopeful
clever	sincere
busy	merry
stale	late
early	idle
useful	new
doubtful	pretty
frightening	obscure
tall	careful
beautiful	suitable
far	tender
gorgeous	intelligent
scarce	plentiful
loud	noisy
rough	far
Final Score: ____________	Final Score: ____________

How many points did you get?
17–18/18 (Excellent!) 15/18 (Well done!) 9/18 (Oops! Read the rules again!)

Aufgabe 7 For your job with New Musical Express you have been asked to review two albums for the magazine's Top 100 albums ever made. The two albums are Van Morrison's 'Hymns to the Silence' and 'No Need to Argue' by The Cranberries. Take the following information and complete the report in which you compare the two.

Van Morrison has been on the music scene (long) (1) ________ the Cranberries and his album 'Hymns to the Silence' appeared three years (early) (2) ________ 'No Need To Argue'. It is both (lively) (3) ________________ and (expensive) (4) ___________ the Limerick group's album and, some critics would say, much (good) (5) ___________. For a start it has (many) (6) ______________ tracks (7) ___________ its counterpart. The Cranberries have only 13 tracks on their album, Van Morrison has almost twice as many. That said, the best song on 'No Need To Argue', a track entitled Zombie, is (famous) (8) ______________ and much (good) (9) ________________ any song on 'Hymns to the Silence'. In addition, a number of songs on 'Hymns to the Silence' are weak, much (bad) (10) ___________ any song on 'No Need to Argue'. However, because it is a double album, 'Hymns to the Silence' is (good) (11) ___________ value, (interesting) (12) ______________ and (satisfying) (13) ______________ the (short) (14) ____________ ,(superficial) (15) ___________ 'No Need to Argue'.

Aufgabe 8 Choose the answer you agree with and complete the sentence by changing the word in brackets. Where there are only two choices you must compare them.

a)

(good) ______________ is the ______________ film of the three.

b)

(interesting) ______________ is the ______________ book I've read in the last while.

c)

(elegant) ______________ was the ______________ dancer in this group.

d)

(tasty) ______________ is a ______________ dish ________ ______________

e)

- Gandhi
- Kennedy
- Reagan

(inspiring) ________________ is the ________________ speaker I ever heard.

e)

- to fail an exam
- to get no birthday presents
- to lose your wallet

(disappointing) ________________ is the ________________ thing that can happen you.

g)

(sweet) ________________ are the ________________ of these fruits.

… rund ums Verb

3 Adverbien

Adverbien sind Wörter wie *always, sometimes, quickly*. Sie bestimmen das im Satz genannte Geschehen in Bezug auf die **Zeit**, den **Raum**, die **Qualität** und die **Intensität** näher.

Beispiele:

Beispiele:	He came home today.	(Zeit)
	The girls ran forward.	(Raum)
	Our goalie played well yesterday.	(Qualität)
	The politician spoke passionately.	(Intensität)

3.1 Einsatzmöglichkeiten von Adverbien

Wann verwendest du Adverbien?

Während Adjektive ein Nomen oder ein Pronomen näher bestimmen, werden durch **Adverbien Verben**, **Adjektive**, andere **Adverbien** und sogar ganze **Sätze** näher beschrieben.

Beispiele:
The policeman moved cautiously.
(nähere Bestimmung eines Verbs)
Helen was fairly satisfied with her results.
(nähere Bestimmung eines Adjektivs)
Ann sang quite beautifully.
(nähere Bestimmung eines Adverbs)
Surely you've brought enough money to pay for the meal.
(nähere Bestimmung eines Satzes)

Wie bildest du Adverbien?

- Die meisten Adverbien bildest du, indem du *-ly* an das entsprechende Adjektiv anhängst.
  Beispiel: slow → slowly
- Du formst Adjektive, die auf einen Konsonanten + *-le* enden, um, indem du *-e* durch *-y* ersetzt.
  Beispiel: sensible → sensibly

- Bei Adjektiven, die auf -y enden, ersetzt du -y durch *-i* und hängst *-ly* an.
  Beispiel: gay → gaily
- Bei Adjektiven, die auf *-ll* enden, hängst du -y an.
  Beispiel: full → fully
- Bei Adjektiven, die auf *-ic* enden, verwandelst du das *-ic* in *-ically*.
  Beispiel: automatic → automatically
- Von Adjektiven, die auf *-ly* enden, kannst du keine Adverbien bilden, du musst eine **adverbiale Bestimmung** (meist mit dem Zusatz *way*) daraus machen.
  Beispiel: He is a friendly man. → He speaks in a friendly way.
- Ausnahmen: unregelmäßige Adverbienbildung.
  Beispiel: good → well
- Ausnahmen: Adjektive und Adverbien, die die gleiche Form haben.

Beispiele:	hard → hard		wrong → wrong	
	high → high		far → far	
	early → early		short → short	
	pretty → pretty		low → low etc.	

Aufgabe 1 Your task here is to form adverbs from the adjectives in the list.

a) miserable ____________ b) extreme ____________
c) sublime ____________ d) happy ____________
e) merciful ____________ f) intolerable ____________

Aufgabe 2 Here you must replace the underlined words with one adverb.

Many people are of the opinion that the Tory Party ruled Britain in a fair way (1) (________) from 1979 onwards. Margaret Thatcher, Tory supporters would claim, lead the nation with great skill (2) (__________). Other British people approach this topic with caution (3) (__________). For them the Tory Party treated people such as the miners and the H-Block strikers in a cruel way (4) (________). They speak with great anger (5) (__________) when the name Thatcher is mentioned in conversation. They see how Conservative supporters live in comfort (6) (_________) in large detached houses while many Labour Party supporters live in small terraced houses and are quite poor. At regular times (7) (___________) they hear stories about rich Tories who have gained further wealth through power and connections. As the general election approaches it seems such people will at last (8) (_____________) have a new non-Tory government which will do more for the poor of Britain and not treat them in a cruel way (9) (_____________).

An welche Stelle im Satz stellst du Adverbien?

- Adverbien, die Verben näher bestimmen, haben keine feste Stellung im Satz. Sie können daher am **Anfang** eines Satzes stehen, in der **Mitte** oder auch am **Ende**. Die Positionierung hängt davon ab, wie stark du das Adverb **betonen** möchtest.

  Beispiele: Wearily, he climbed into bed.
  (Anfang des Satzes, starke Betonung)
  He climbed wearily into bed.
  (Mitte des Satzes, Adverb wird nicht betont)
  He climbed into bed wearily.
  (Ende des Satzes, starke Betonung)

- Allgemein kann man sagen, dass das **Adverb nach dem Verb bzw. nach dem Objekt** kommt. Auf keinen Fall darfst du das Adverb aber zwischen Verb und direktes Objekt stellen.

  Beispiel: I like tea very much.

- Manche Adverbien werden aber **vor das Verb** gestellt. Darunter: *still, just, already, frequently, seldom, always, often, rarely, sometimes, generally, usually, never, partly, hardly, scarcely, yet, only.*

  Beispiel: I just called to say hello.

- Taucht ein **Adverb innhalb einer *verb phrase*** auf, steht es in der Regel nach dem ersten Wort.

  Beispiel: The death might possibly have been avoided if …

- Enthält ein Satz **mehrere Adverbien** oder **adverbiale Bestimmungen**, so lautet die Reihenfolge:
  1. Manner, 2. Place, 3. Time

  Beispiel: Ronaldo played well at Anfield last year.

- Enthält ein Satz **mehrere Zeitadverbien**, wird **das genauere Adverb vor das allgemeinere** gestellt.

  Beispiel: He got married at one o'clock on Valentine's Day in 2001.

Aufgabe 3 Place the words in the brackets in the right place. Sometimes two or more answers are possible. Name the country!

a) Conversation plays an important part in daily life here. (still)
b) A woman has been Prime Minister of this country. (never)
c) One particular woman, Maire Geoghegan-Quinn, has retired from politics after twenty years service. (just)
d) The country is enjoying an increased standard of living thanks to tourism and EC membership. (currently)
e) The country wins major sporting events. (rarely)
f) Farming remains important in this land. (vitally)

g) The people enjoy traditional sports such as hurling. (very much)
h) In 2003 people flocked to see a film about Veronica Guerin. (to the cinemas)
i) Radio talkshows such as Marion Finucane's Liveline are popular there. (immensely)
j) In 2003, Eoin Colfer's third 'Artemis Fowl' book was received by the critics. (good)
k) Aer Lingus, the national airline, flies people to and from Germany. (regularly)
l) This ultra-Catholic nation voted in favour of divorce in 1995. (finally)

Name of the country: ______________________

Aufgabe 4 Again you have to place the adverbs in the right place. Only this time it's a famous film you're trying to uncover. Sometimes more than one answer is possible.

a) This movie has been called a blockbuster of a film. (often)
b) It was directed by Steven Spielberg. (brilliantly)
c) It was conceived by George Lucas. (in the 1970s)
d) The music for the film was composed by John Williams. (carefully)
e) Karen Allen plays the leading lady in the film. (beautifully)
f) The storyline develops and centres around a freelance treasure hunter who is searching for something. (quickly, desperately)
g) Harrison Ford performs as the main character. (powerfully)
h) The sequel to this film was dramatic and was called Indiana Jones and the Temple of Doom. (equally)

Name of the film: ________________________________

3.2 Adverbien – Steigerung und Vergleiche

Wann steigerst du Adverbien und wann verwendest du Vergleiche?

Für Adverbien gelten hier dieselben Regeln wie für Adjektive (siehe S. 22/23).

Beispiele: He contributed most generously to the Labour Party. (Steigerung)
Theo dresses more fashionably than Eileen. (Vergleich)

Wie bildest du Steigerungsformen der Adverbien und wie bildest du Vergleiche?

Auch hierfür gelten dieselben Regeln wie für Adjektive (siehe S. 22/23).

Aufgabe 5 Test yourself! Give the adverbs of these adjectives – and their comparative and superlative forms!

a) early ______ ______ ______

b) safe ______ ______ ______

c) intensive ______ ______ ______

d) sure ______ ______ ______

e) fortunate ______ ______ ______

f) sensible ______ ______ ______

g) high ______ ______ ______

h) deserved ______ ______ ______

i) jolly ______ ______ ______

j) similiar ______ ______ ______

k) true ______ ______ ______

l) deep ______ ______ ______

m) whole ______ ______ ______

Aufgabe 6 Complete the sentences.

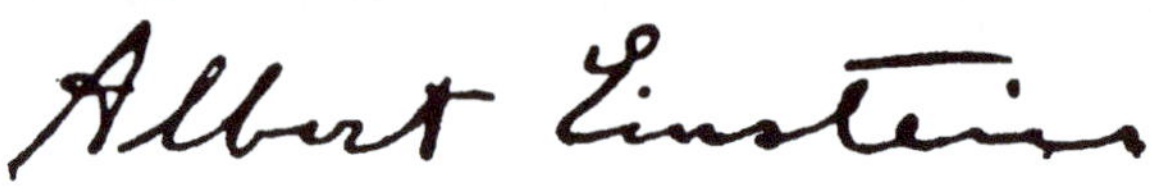

Did you know that Einstein did (1) ______________ (badly) than most of the students in the entrance exam for the Technical Institute in Zurich? Two years later he performed (2) ______________ (well) than that and was accepted.
Many men he knew worked hard. For years Einstein worked (3) ______________ (hard) of all as he tried to finish his theory. Having started work on it in the 1880s, he completed it much (4) ______________ (late) in 1915.
Did you know that Einstein played the violin? He didn't play (5) ______________ (badly) either. In fact some musicians thought he played the violin (6) ______________ (beautifully) than many professionals they knew.
People in the science world praised him (7) ______________ (energetically) of all but ordinary people thought (8) ______________ (highly) of him too!

Aufgabe 7 In the following exercise you will learn something about The Farmers' Market in Kitchener, Canada. It is the place where people come "to find the best of the best" according to one market vendor. Your task is to complete the sentences with the correct comparative or superlative forms.

The vendors at the Kitchener Farmers' Market sell fruit and vegetables (cheap) (1) more cheaply ______ than the supermarkets do. Early on Saturday morning or sometimes the night before, the vendors set up their stalls (careful and beautiful) (2) ______ any vendors I know. If you ask me they are the people who work (efficient) (3) ______ of all the workers in town. Of all the vendors the ones who add (delightful) (4) ______ to the flair of the market are the arts and craft vendors who often work (hard) (5) ______ all the rest creating products on the spot for customers at their stall. There is no doubt but that these local producers can get their products (fast) (6) ______ to your shopping basket than any supermarket chain can. The local customers arrive at the market (early) (7) ______ those who travel in from Waterloo County or from housing estates in the suburbs. It is possible that the vendors welcome local people (warm) (8) ______ of all but they try to make tourists feel at home too. The vendors sell their huge choice of foods, including fruits and vegetables such as sauerkraut, radishes, pickles, cauliflower and plums (quick) (9) ______ those selling items such as quilts and rugs. For the tourist it would be better if some vendors spoke (clear) (10) ______ as their local dialect can sometimes cause problems. Certain names of goods sold at the market contribute (significant) (11) ______ of all to the magic of the Farmers' Market in Kitchener. These include pussywillows, maple syrup and samosas. The (old) (12) ______ the market gets the (famous) (13) ______ it becomes. The Farmers' Market has been operating (continuous) (14) continuously ______ since 1869!

Now starring…
Depending on the season, at the Kitchener Farmers' Market you can enjoy:
apples · arts · asparagus · beans · beef · beets · blueberries · bread · broccoli · beef · cabbage
cakes · candy · carrots · cauliflower · celery · cheese · cherries · chicken · coffee · cookies · corn
crafts · cream · cucumbers · deli meats · donuts · eggs · fish · flowers · fudge · goatmeat
grapes · herbs · honey · jams · jellies · juices · lamb · lettuce · maple syrup · melons · muffins
nuts · onions · pasta · pastries · peaches · pears · peas · peppers · pickles · pierogies · pies
plants · plums · pork · potatoes · preserves · pretzels · pumpkins · pussywillows · rabbit
radishes · raspberries · refreshments · rhubarb · ribs · rolls · samosas · sauerkraut · sausage
shoo-fly pie · spices · spinach · squash · strawberries · tomatoes · turkey · turnip · veal · zucchini
Quality & Freshness
Kitchener Farmers' Market
Saturday markets open year-round, 6 am to 2 pm
Corner of Frederick and Duke Streets, downtown Kitchener
Telephone: (519)741-2287 Fax: (519)741-2767
FOODLAND ONTARIO

3.3 Adverb oder Adjektiv?

Wann verwendest du ein Adjektiv und wann ein Adverb?

Es ist wichtig, genau zwischen Adverbien und Adjektiven zu unterscheiden. Ihre Funktion im Satz ist verschieden.

Beispiel: Harry looked happy.
(*happy* beschreibt in diesem Beispiel Harry.)
Harry looked happily at the birthday cake.
(Hier beschreibt *happily*, wie Harry seinen Kuchen anschaut.)

Oftmals sehen sich aber Adverbien und Adjektive sehr ähnlich, unterscheiden sich in ihrer Bedeutung aber ganz und gar. In solchen Fällen musst du besonders gut aufpassen, dass du Adverb und Adjektiv nicht verwechselst.

Beispiel: Jim has just come home. He was justly given four years in prison.

Aufgabe 8 Find the adjectives. There are quite a lot of adjectives in the following text. Can you find them. Be careful! There are also a lot of adverbs there!

TV soap operas are extremely popular in Britain. Programmes such as *East-enders, Neighbours* and *Born and Bred* are well-produced and attract large audiences according to the experts who study the television ratings closely. There are, however, people who consider these programmes awful. Whenever I feel tired I like to watch *Casualty,* a relatively new series. No matter how sad the story is one can be quietly confident of a gripping end. The most famous single programme from any TV series shown in Britain was the *Who shot J. R.?* episode of *Dallas* back in the early years of soap operas. It all seems incredible now but when it was shown it kept the entire county guessing, waiting impatiently for the answer. Everyone made a straight line for their TV sets when the programme started. Because we receive more and more TV channels every year it is fairly difficult to choose which soap operas to watch. If soap operas don't catch on fast they are usually dropped by the TV stations.

Aufgabe 9 In this exercise you have to decide which of the two words to use. On a number of occasions both words have to be used.

(1) ________________ (late/lately), many British people have begun to question the value of the monarchy. A recent study looked (2) ________________ (close/closely) at the attitudes of people throughout the United Kingdom. It came to the (3) ________________ (hard/hardly) surprising conclusion that attitudes are at (4) ________________ (last/lastly) changing. The popularity of the House of Windsor has been (5) ________________ hit by the (6)

_______________ (bad/badly) publicity Prince Charles has received. While many English people love the crown (7) _______________ (dear/dearly) there are just as many Scots, Liverpudlians and Northern Irish nationalists to name but a few for whom the monarchy is (8) _______________ (simple/simply) too (9) _______________ (dear/dearly) to justify keeping the Royal Family any longer. The recent dispute over a new Royal yacht was just the tip of the iceberg for many who are calling for a more (10) _______________ (just/justly) system. In their eyes a republic might be a better alternative and one that would treat everyone (11) _______________ (fair/fairly) and (12) _______________ (just/justly). A couple of years ago the monarchy had a (13) _______________ (close/closely) shave with[1] disaster when its ratings plummeted[2] in the wake of the Charles and Diana divorce. Many ordinary English people remain (14) _______________ (high/highly) amused by the Royals and their antics. They provide them with juicy stories and are good for tourism. Newspaper editors would be lost without the Royal family who keep circulation figures (15) _______________ (high/highly). The Prime Minister is expected to speak to the nation (16) _______________ on the matter of the monarchy and after his speech journalists will be allowed time for a few (17) _______________ questions (short/shortly). The Royals have to be very (18) _______________ guarded (close/closely). For instance, on a recent (19) _______________ delivery for Prince Harry it (20) _______________ stated that the receiver was to pay the postage (expressly/express). This made a security official (21) _______________ (wary/warily) and the parcel had to be examined by bomb disposal experts[3]. It remains to be seen what long-term effects the tragic death of Diana, Princess of Wales, will have on Britain's most famous institution.

1 a close shave with: almost, nearly ran into disaster
2 its ratings plummeted – the poularity of the monarchy dropped
3 bomb disposal experts – people who make bombs safe

Aufgabe 10 **Revision exercise:** Adjectives and adverbs. You and Your Money

Your task is to decide whether an adjective or an adverb is required to complete the sentence. Then fill in the gap with the adjective from the list or change it to an adverb if necessary!

proper, incredible, foolish, friendly, instant, angry, serious, home-based, bad, happy, good, complete, probable, expensive, regular, terrible, monthly, close, fast, close, wise, careful

Did you know that most grown-ups are unable to look after their money (1) __________? They do this not, as you might think, by spending it (2) __________ but by not knowing how to manage their incomes (3) __________.
Geoffrey Holland is an Australian (4) __________ financial adviser. In the course of his job he (5) __________ sees examples of (6) __________ mismanagement. "Most people are (7) incredibly disorganized" he claims. "Ask them what their (8) __________ electricity bill is and they (9) __________ can't tell you. Many of them are (10) __________ controlled by their credit cards. Yet they sound (11) __________ when I tell them this on the phone. I explain to them that if they can't pay off their bill at the end of the month they should get rid of the card (12) __________." I also ask people to note down (13) __________ every item they purchase over a couple of months and then take a (14) __________ look at their tax arrangements, insurance plans, savings, loans and other financial business. This is something Helen and Fritz felt they (15) __________ needed to do. (16) __________ and hard-working, both hold down good jobs, they have five demanding and (17) __________ children and an overdraft that (18) __________ worries them. When Geoffrey asked them if they had ever kept a comprehensive record of all the items they bought they said no. After they had examined their financial situation (19) __________ with Geoffrey they opened a joint account, closed their single accounts and started using their money more (20) __________ to pay back loans (21) __________. They are very (22) __________ with their new situation. "People just don't realize how important it is to get control of their money before their money gets control of them" says Helen.

Aufgabe 11 **Revision exercise:** In the following poem by Louis MacNeice (1907–63) your task is to state what each underlined word is (e.g. adjective, preposition, adverb, verb): If you're not sure check back over the chapters you've done so far!

Autobiography

In my childhood trees were green __________
And there was plenty to be seen. __________

Come back early or never come. __________

My father made the walls resound
He wore his collar the wrong way round. __________

Come back early or never come.

My mother wore a yellow dress
Gently, gently, gentleness. ______________________

Come back early or never come.

When I was five the black dreams came,
Nothing after was quite the same. __________ __________

Come back early or never come.

The dark was talking to the dead __________ __________
The lamp was dark beside my bed. __________ __________

Come back early or never come.

When I woke they did not care;
Nobody, nobody was there.

Come back early or never come.

When my silent terror cried ______________________
Nobody, nobody replied.

Come back early or never come.

I got up; the chilly sun ______________________
Saw me walk away alone. ______________________

Come back early or never come.

(Louis MacNeice: Collected Poems. Faber and Faber, London)

Aufgabe 12*

Creative Writing

Ten months ago this dog, a stray, turned up at Patricia's door. When nobody answered her advertisement in the newspaper she decided to keep him. Pretend you are Patricia, or her daughter Tara. Write a summary of how the dog has changed your life, what he means to you and what you feel about dogs in general. Use as many adjectives and adverbs as possible.

4 Zeitformen des Verbs

Die Zeitformen *(tenses)* der Verben entsprechen nicht unmittelbar dem, was wir normalerweise unter Zeit *(time)* verstehen. Sie drücken weder absolute Zeitpunkte aus, noch sind sie in der Lage, über die genaue Dauer eines Geschehens zu informieren. Die **grammatischen Zeitformen der Verben** setzen **Handlungen** und **Ereignisse** lediglich in **Beziehung** zu dem Zeitpunkt, in dem der Sprecher spricht **(Sprechzeitpunkt)**.

Will man von **zurückliegenden Handlungen** berichten, so benutzt man eine **Zeitform der Vergangenheit**. **Gleichzeitig** zum Sprechzeitpunkt stattfindende Ereignisse werden in einer **Form der Gegenwart** formuliert. Wenn man von **kommenden Ereignissen** sprechen will, muss man eine **Form der Zukunft** wählen.

In jeder der drei **Zeitstufen** (Vergangenheit, Gegenwart, Zukunft) stehen uns **verschiedene Zeitformen *(tenses)*** zur Verfügung, mit denen wir die **Art und Weise** von Geschehen ausdrücken können:

- ein Geschehen tritt gerade ein,
- es befindet sich im Verlauf,
- es ist bereits abgeschlossen,
- es hat Auswirkungen auf die Gegenwart

  etc.

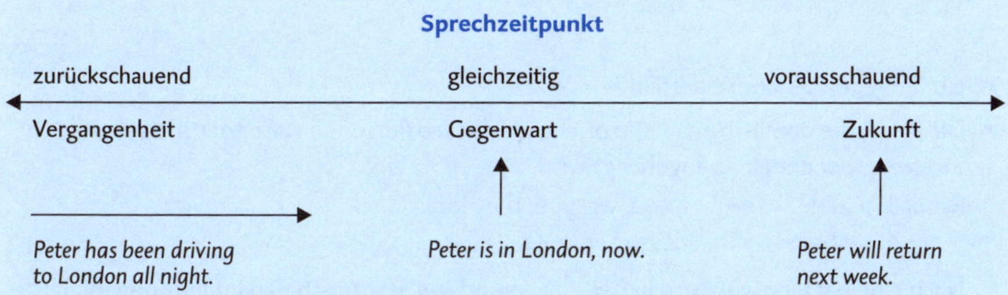

Die Tatsache, dass Peter die ganze Nacht gefahren ist **(andauernde Handlung in der Vergangenheit)**, hat **Auswirkungen auf die Gegenwart**: Peter ist jetzt **(gleichzeitig zum Sprechzeitpunkt)** in London. Nächste Woche **(Blick in die Zukunft)** wird er zurückkommen.

4.1 *simple present* und *present progressive*

Simple present und *present progressive* sind beide **Zeiten der Gegenwart.** Mit ihnen kann man unterschiedliche Arten von Geschehnissen bzw. Handlungen ausdrücken.

Rund ums *simple present*

Wann verwendest du das *simple present?*

- Mit dem *simple present* drückt man **Gewohnheiten** aus: Etwas geschieht **regelmäßig, oft, manchmal** oder **nie.**
  Signalwörter hierfür sind *every day, never, from time to time, usually, sometimes, seldom, rarely, always, on Mondays* etc.
  Beispiel: I get up at 5.30 on Mondays.
- Das *simple present* steht auch bei **allgemein gültigen Tatsachen.**
  Beispiel: The river flows to the sea.
- **Handlungsfolgen**, bei denen die **Dauer keine Rolle spielt**, stehen ebenfalls im *simple present.*
  Beispiel: Harry enters the room, closes the door and sits down.

Wie bildest du das *simple present?*

- Die Form, die dem **Infinitiv** entspricht, gilt für alle Personen außer der **3. Person Singular**, bei der ein ***-s*** angehängt wird.
  Beispiel: look → I, you, we, you, they look
  aber: he, she, it looks
- Nach einem **Zischlaut** wird in der **3. Person Singular *-es*** an den Infinitiv angehängt.
  Beispiele: press → he, she, it presses
  push → he, she, it pushes
  catch → he, she, it catches
  box → he, she, it boxes
- Bei der 3. Person Singular wird -y nach Konsonant zu *-ies.*
  Beispiel: cry → he, she, it cries
- Merke dir die folgenden **drei Sonderfälle** bei der **3. Person Singular:**
  do → he, she, it does
  go → he, she, it goes
  say → he, she, it says

Tonguetwister

If you want to remember the *-s* in the third person singular try learning this tonguetwister by heart and then see if your friends can say it!

Aufgabe 1* Proverbs and sayings often use the *simple present*. Can you work out what proverbs are pictured here?

a)

Money ____

b)

All ____

c)

What goes ______________________________

d)

The early ______________________________

Aufgabe 2 You are staying with your pen-pal, Helen Blackmore, in Brighton. Some things about her family strike you as very strange and very English. Write a letter home about your impressions. Include all the information shown in the pictures.

Dear Mam,

How are you all? I have settled in well and am enjoying myself. Helen and her family are nice to me. Mind you, you wouldn't believe some of the things they do and that happen here. For instance:

- Helen wears a uniform to school.

  All the students have to wear one. How awful!

- …
- …
- …
- …
- …
- …
- …

Love,

…

Rund ums *present progressive*

Wann verwendest du das *present progressive?*

Das *present progressive* beschreibt **Tätigkeiten** und **Vorgänge**, die **noch nicht abgeschlossen** sind. Diese Zeitstufe drückt meistens aus, dass jemand gerade dabei ist, etwas zu tun.
Signalwörter für den Gebrauch des *present progressive* sind *now, just, at the moment, at present* etc.

Beispiel: We are living in rented accomodation at present.

Die meisten Verben, die **keine Tätigkeits-** (z. B. *run, sing, play, walk*) **oder Vorgangsverben** (z. B. *become, rain, snow*) sind, können **nicht in der *progressive*-Form** stehen (z. B. *notice, hear, think, believe*).

Wie bildest du das *present progressive?*

- Präsens-Form von ***to be* + *ing*-Form des Verbs**

  Beispiel: I am playing
  you/we/they are playing
  he/she/it is playing

- **Nach kurzem, betonten Vokal** wird der **Endkonsonant verdoppelt**.

  Beispiel: cut → cutting

- Stummes **-*e* am Ende entfällt**.

  Beispiel: whine → whining

- **-*ie* am Ende** wird zu **-*y***.

  Beispiel: lie → lying

Aufgabe 3 All of the following are happening right now in the Fishburn house. They are getting ready to go on holidays to Germany. Write a sentence to match each square.

a)

The dog is running off with the map.
Mr Fishburn ______________________________

____

b) 

Tom ____

____

c) 

Lucy ____

____

d) 

Catherine ____

____

e) 

Grandad ____

____

f) 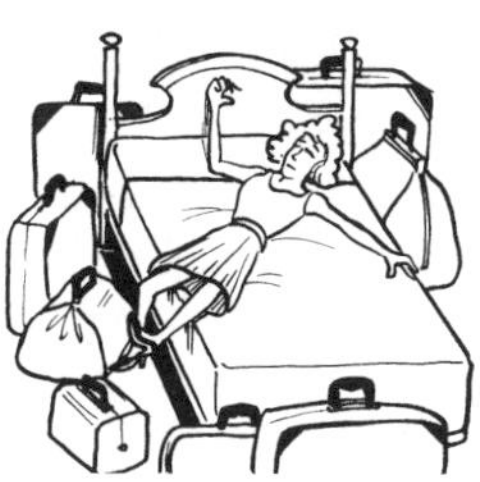

Mrs Fishburn ____

____

Aufgabe 4 **Mixed exercise:** *simple present* or *present progressive?* Put in the correct form of the verb.

a) C.I.E.'s Expressway Bus from Waterford to Dublin ______________ (to leave) Plunkett Station at 8.30 every morning.

b) It's 8.20 and the passengers ______________ (to board) the bus.

c) It's the driver's job ______________ (to give) them their tickets and ______________ (to store) any luggage in a safe place. He often ______________ (to greet) them with a smile.

d) Usually people ______________ (to read), ______________ (to eat) or ______________ (to sleep) if the person next to them ______________ (to have) very little to say.

e) At the moment the passengers ______________ (to listen) to the Gerry Ryan show on 2 FM which can be heard on loudspeakers in the bus.

f) Now and then an inspector ______________ (to stop) the bus and ______________ (to check) that everything is in order.

4.2 *simple past* und *past progressive*

Simple past und *past progressive* sind beide **Zeiten der Vergangenheit** und drücken **unterschiedliche Arten von vergangenen Handlungen bzw. Ereignissen** aus.

Rund ums *simple past*

Wann verwendest du das *simple past?*

- Mit dem *simple past* drückt man **Handlungen** und **Vorgänge** aus, **die in der Vergangenheit abgeschlossen** sind.
  Signalwörter hierfür sind *yesterday, last night, last year, … ago, in 1946* etc.
  Beispiel: World War I broke out in 1914.
- **Handlungen** und **Vorgänge**, die **in der Vergangenheit aufeinanderfolgten**, stehen ebenfalls im *simple past*. Deshalb ist das *simple past* auch die **typische Zeitform von Erzählungen**.
  Beispiel: Hey diddle diddle,
  The cat and the fiddle
  The cow jumped over the moon;
  The little dog laughed to see such fun
  And the dish ran away with the spoon.

Wie bildest du das *simple past?*

- Bei **regelmäßigen Verben** wird die Endung ***-ed* an den Infinitiv** angehängt.
  Beispiel: work → I, you, he, she, it, we, you, they worked
- **Nach Konsonanten** wird **-y** zu ***-ie***.
  Beipiele: bury → buried
  carry → carried
- **Nach** kurzem **betonten Vokal** wird der **Endkonsonant verdoppelt**.
  Beipiel: stop → stopped
- Viele Verben haben **unregelmäßige Formen in der Vergangenheit**. Du musst sie **auswendig lernen**.
  Beispiel: give → gave
  go → went

Aufgabe 5 Using the correct verb that fits the sentence make full sentences to write the biography of this famous person and work out who it is: to die, to write, to be born, to graduate from, to join, to run, to get, to fight, to beat, to marry

a) 1917 / Brookline, USA
I was born in Brookline, USA in 1917.

b) 1940 / Harvard University
____

c) 1940 / the book "Why England Slept"
____

d) 1941 / the navy and / in World War 2
____

e) 1946 / for Congress
____

f) 1953 / Jackie
____

g) 1960 / Richard Nixon
____

h) 1963 / in my wife's arms
____

My name: ____________________

Aufgabe 6 For the next exercise you have to become a poet! Finish this poem by putting in the past tense simple form of the verb in brackets.

A Fairy Went A-Marketing

A fairy ________________ a-marketing (to go)
She ________________ a little fish (to buy)
She ________________ it in a crystal bowl (to put)
Upon a golden dish.
An hour she ________________ in wonderment (to sit)
And ________________ its silver gleam (to watch)
And then she gently ________________ it up (to take)
And ________________ it in a stream. (to slip)
A fairy ________________ a-marketing (to go)
She ________________ a gentle mouse (to buy)
To take her tiny messages
To keep her little house.
All day she ________________ its busy feet (to keep)
Pit-patting to and fro
And then she ________________ its silken ears (to kiss)
________________ it and ________________ it go. (to thank) (to let)

(by Rose Fyleman, Fairies and Chimneys)

Rund ums *past progressive*

Wann verwendest du das *past progressive?*

Man verwendet das *past progressive*, um zu beschreiben, **was gerade geschah, als eine andere Handlung eintrat**. Das *past progressive* ist die Zeitstufe der **Hintergrundhandlungen**.
Signalwörter für den Gebrauch des *past progressive* sind *just then, at that moment, while, when, always* etc.

Beispiel: Mammy was making bread when the phone rang.

Wie bildest du das *past progressive?*

***past*-Form** von ***to be* + *ing*-Form des Verbs**

Beispiel: I, he, she, it was/you, we, they were working

Es gelten dieselben **Sonderfälle für die *ing*-Endung wie im *present progressive*** (siehe S. 44).

Aufgabe 7 Last year a number of students were travelling across Britain when their train came to an abrupt stop just outside Cambridge. Your task is to describe what they were doing when the train stopped.

a) 

Suzi from Bristol: "The moment the train stopped I was drying my hair."

b) 

Jane and Simon from Aldershot: "______________________________."

c)

Anna from Madrid: "____."

d)

Fleming from Copenhagen: "____."

e)

Jean from Paris: "____."

f)

Sinéad from Sligo: "____."

g)

Wolfgang from Hof: "____."

h)

Gabor from Budapest: "____."

i)

Tom from Boston: "____."

4.3 *present perfect simple* und *progressive*

Present perfect simple und *progressive* sind genau wie *simple past* und *past progressive* beide **Zeitstufen der Vergangenheit** und drücken **unterschiedliche Arten von vergangenen Handlungen bzw. Ereignissen** aus.

Rund ums *present perfect simple*

Wann verwendest du das *present perfect simple?*

- Das *present perfect simple* wird gebraucht, um Handlungen zu beschreiben, die **in der Vergangenheit begonnen** haben und **bis zum Zeitpunkt des Sprechens andauern**.

  Beispiel: Tom has only lived here for a month. He hardly knows anyone jet.

- Es beschreibt auch Handlungen, die zwar vorüber sind, jedoch **Auswirkungen auf die Gegenwart** haben.

  Beispiel: I haven't written any Christmas cards yet. I must do that today.

Signalwörter für den Gebrauch des *present perfect simple* sind *so far, yet, already, just, by now, since, ever.*

Wie bildest du das *present perfect simple?*

have/has + past participle

Beispiel: I, you, we, they have/he, she, it has played

Regelmäßig wird das *past participle* auf **-ed** gebildet, wobei dieselben Regeln gelten wie für die Bildung des *past tense* auf *-ed* (vgl. S. 47).

Die **unregelmäßigen Verben** (sowohl *past*-Form als auch *past participle*) musst du **auswendig lernen.**

If you want to remember …

Aufgabe 8* What has happened here? Describe how the Fishburns are getting on during the holiday. Write a postcard to a friend at home. Use the present perfect simple and progressive. Mention any other things you think might have happened. Tell the person you're writing to when you'll be home.

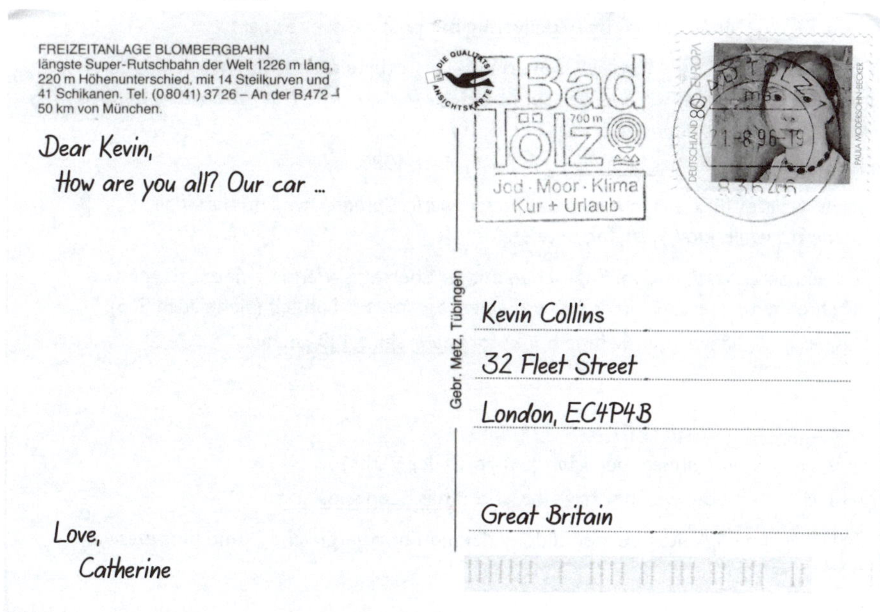
FREIZEITANLAGE BLOMBERGBAHN
längste Super-Rutschbahn der Welt 1226 m läng,
220 m Höhenunterschied, mit 14 Steilkurven und
41 Schikanen. Tel. (08041) 3726 – An der B472 –
50 km von München.

Dear Kevin,
How are you all? Our car ...

Love,
Catherine

Bad Tölz
700 m
Jod · Moor · Klima
Kur + Urlaub

Gebr. Metz, Tübingen

Kevin Collins
32 Fleet Street
London, EC4P4B

Great Britain

Aufgabe 9 **Globetrotter Club:** Anyone who can call themselves a globetrotter has been to many countries. Can you figure out the countries this particular globetrotter has been to? Use the verbs in brackets.

a) I have ______________ (to walk) from Land's End to John O'Groats.
Ah! So you ______________ (to be) to ______________ then.

b) I ______________ (to stand) on top of Ayers Rock.
That means you ______________ (to visit) ______________.

c) I ______________ (to watch) tennis in Flushing Meadows.
Really? You ______________ (to attend) the ______________ Open?

d) I ______________ (to swim) in Lake Winnipeg.
You must ______________ (to spend) time in ______________ then.

e) I ______________ (to sleep) in a hotel in Cagliari.
Well, you ______________ (to see) ______________ then!

Rund ums *present perfect progressive*

Wann verwendest du das *present perfect progressive?*

Das *present perfect progressive* betont – im Gegensatz zum *present perfect simple* – die **Dauer der Handlung** bzw. **des Vorgangs**.

Beispiele: I have been waiting for the bus for an hour.
Mr Major has been delivering our post for over 5 years.

Folgende **Verben, die einen längeren Vorgang** oder eine **immer wiederholte Handlung beschreiben**, werden sehr **häufig im *present perfect progressive*** benutzt:
sit, live, stay, stand, hang, wait, spend, work, try usw.

Beispiel: Helen has been living in Spain since 1986.

Signalwörter für den Gebrauch des *present perfect progressive* sind *the whole …, for the last while, lately, just, for, since* etc.

Das deutsche **‚seit'** wird im Englischen mit ***for*** übersetzt, wenn es eine **Zeitspanne** beschreibt, mit ***since***, wenn es sich um einen **Zeitpunkt** handelt (siehe auch S. 6).

Beispiel: I have been writing books for years, since 1991 in fact.

Wie bildest du das *present perfect progressive?*

have/has + been + present participle (*ing*-Form des Verbs)

Beispiel: I, you, we, they have/he, she, it has been speaking

Zu Unregelmäßigkeiten bei der Bildung der *ing*-Form vergleiche „Rund ums *present progressive*", S. 44.

Aufgabe 10 Put the verbs in brackets into the present perfect progressive.

a) I ________________ (to work) in Ingolstadt since 1972.

b) How long you ________________ (to learn) French?

c) The baby ________________ (to sleep) all morning.

d) We ________________ (to spend) too much money on clothes lately.

e) The clothes ________________ (to lie) on the table for days.

Aufgabe 11 **Revision exercise:** Fill in the missing verbs in the correct tense and find out more about Ontario! Use simple present, present perfect, or simple past!

The province of Ontario in Canada (1) ____________ (to be) a traveller's paradise for many years. Its most famous natural asset, Niagara Falls, (2) ____________ (to attract) visitors from all over the world for as long as anybody can recall. Charles Dickens, the well-known English writer, (3) ____________ (to come) here in 1842. Over the years many people (4) ____________ (to try) going over the Falls but very few (5) ____________ (to survive) the trip. The first person who lived to tell the tale (6) ____________ (to be) a schoolteacher who, in 1901, (7) ____________ (to go) over the Falls in a barrel! Niagara Falls (8) ____________ (to remain) one of the great natural wonders of the world and 12 million people (9) ____________ (to come) to look at it every year. Last week a friend of mine (10) ____________ (to amaze) me by claiming that the largest game preserve in the world (11) ____________ (to be) not in Africa but in Ontario. Not only that but Ontario (12) ____________ (to boast) half a million lakes! Huge retreating glaciers (13) ____________ (to cut) out these lakes thousands of years ago and today they (14) ____________ (to provide) the tourists with wonderful opportunities to go canoeing.
The city of Toronto (15) ____________ (to have) always close contacts with the United States. In 1988 the UN (16) ____________ (to describe) Toronto as the most multicultural city in the world. This (17) ____________ (to make) it an attractive place to visit. Have you ever (18) ____________ (to wish) you could spend the weekend in a lakeside cottage? That (19) ____________ (to be) what a lot of Canadians (20) ____________ (to do) in Ontario each weekend. They (21) ____________ (to fish), (22) ____________ (to hunt), and (23) ____________ (to relax). Over the past few decades Ottawa's Tulip Festival (24) ____________ (to grow) into the largest tulip festival in the world. In 1992 the city (25) ____________ (to celebrate) the 125th anni-

versary of the Confederation. It (26) ______________ (to seem) (27) ______________ (to be) quite a party. It (28) ______________ (to last) 125 days! If ever you (29) ______________ (to visit) Ontario and happen (30) ______________ (to hear) musket fire then you (31) ______________ (to know) you are in Kingston. It (32) ______________ (to have) the honour of being Canada's first capital many years ago and Fort Henry, its renowned fort, still (33) ______________ (to echo) to the sound of canon and musket roar for the benefit of the tourists.

Aufgabe 12 **Vocabulary exercise:** Find out the meaning of the following words.

asset	______________	a barrel	______________
to boast	______________	to retreat	______________
musket	______________	renowned	______________

4.4 *past perfect simple* und *progressive*

Past perfect simple und *progressive* sind genau wie *past* bzw. *present perfect simple* und *progressive* beide **Zeitstufen der Vergangenheit** und drücken wie alle *simple-* und *progressive*-Formen **unterschiedliche Arten von vergangenen Handlungen bzw. Ereignissen** aus.

Rund ums *past perfect simple*

Wann verwendest du das *past perfect simple?*

Das *past perfect* wird gebraucht, um Handlungen oder Vorgänge, die sich in der **Vergangenheit** abgespielt haben, in die richtige zeitliche Reihenfolge zu bringen: **was zuerst passierte**, wird im ***past perfect*** ausgedrückt, was darauf folgte oder **später passierte**, im ***simple past***.

Signalwörter für den Gebrauch des *past perfect simple* sind *already, just, by then, after, when* etc.

Beispiel: We ate breakfast after Sharon had made a pot of tea.

Wie bildest du das *past perfect simple?*

had + past participle

Beispiel: I, you, he, she, it, we, they had played

Regelmäßig wird das *past participle* auf ***-ed*** gebildet, wobei dieselben Regeln gelten wie für die Bildung des *past tense* auf *-ed* (vgl. S. 46).

Die **unregelmäßigen Verben** (sowohl *past*-Form als auch *past participle*) musst du **auswendig lernen**.

Aufgabe 13 Complete the following by placing the verb in the past perfect simple.

a) I ______________ (to read) Translations by Brian Friel before I saw it on stage in Dublin.

b) Tom gave Mary a present for all she ______________ (to do) for him.

c) Conor went to school after he ______________ (to eat) his breakfast.

d) Eilis told me her name after I ______________ (to explain) I could not read it.

e) They drank a cup of coffee after they ______________ (to return) from lunch.

f) The priest received a present from the people for the help he ______________ (to give) them.

g) The queen read her speech after everyone ______________ (to sit) down.

Rund ums *past perfect progressive*

Wann verwendest du das *past perfect progressive?*

Das *past perfect progressive* betont – wie alle *progressive*-Formen – die **Dauer einer Handlung** bzw. **eines Vorgangs**.

Beispiel: Helen had been living in Spain for two years when she met Matt.

Verben, die einen längeren Vorgang oder eine immer wiederholte Handlung beschreiben und die häufig im *present perfect progressive* stehen (vgl. S. 54), stehen auch oft im *past perfect progressive*.
Es gelten auch dieselben Signalwörter wie für den Gebrauch des *present perfect progressive* (vgl. S. 54).

Wie bildest du das *past perfect progressive?*

had been + *present participle* (*ing*-Form des Verbs)

Beispiel: I/you/he/she/it/we/you/they had been climbing

Zu Unregelmäßigkeiten bei der Bildung der *ing*-Form verlgleiche „Rund ums *present progressive*", S. 44.

Aufgabe 14* Your task here is to fill in the missing verbs in either the *past tense simple* or *past perfect* as you see fit.

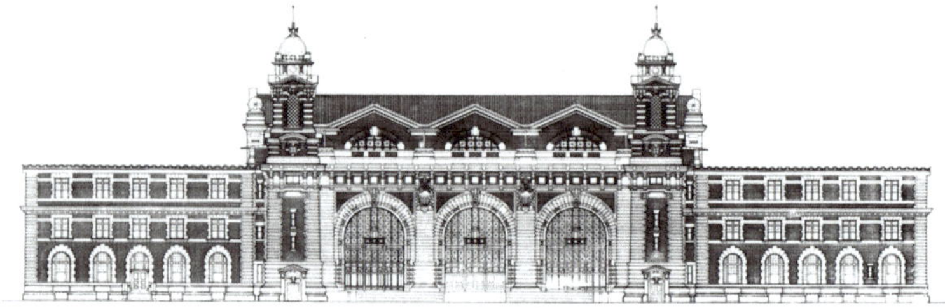

Ellis Island I. For many emigrants who made the journey to America in the 19th century the worst was not the difficult conditions or the 35 dangerous days on board ship but their arrival at Ellis Island, an island off the Manhattan coast.

a) After the island ________________ (to serve) as a fort and execution site it ________________ (to become) an immigration centre in 1892.

b) Between 1892 and 1924 12 million people first ________________ (to set foot) in America at Ellis Island.

c) It ________________ (to be) there in the Great Hall at Ellis Island that doctors and officials ________________ (to decide) the futures of all those who ________________ (to leave) Europe and other areas of the world in the hope of a new life in America.

d) After they ________________ (to pass) through the baggage room, the newcomers ________________ (to climb) a long stairs up to the Great Hall.

e) Once the doctors ________________ (to examine) everybody officials ________________ (to come) and ________________ (to question) them.

f) They were asked if they ______________________ (to be) to America before, if they ______________________ (to pay) for their ticket, if they ______________________ (to work) before, if they ______________________ (to learn) any skills in their own country.

g) After they ____________ (to give) the right answers they ____________ (to head) off in search of the New World.

4.5 *future tenses*

Wann verwendest du *future tenses?*

Es gibt im Englischen **mehrere Zeitformen**, um Vorgänge, die sich in der **Zukunft** abspielen werden, auszudrücken. Welche der Möglichkeiten man wählt, hängt von der jeweiligen **Sprechabsicht** ab.

- Man verwendet das ***will-future*** für **Vorhersagen, spontane Willenserklärungen** und zum Ausdruck von **künftigem Geschehen, das der Sprecher nicht beeinflussen kann**.

  Beispiele: He will arrive by train.
  I will do it myself.
  The company will close next year.

- Das ***going-to-future*** wird verwendet, um **Vorhaben** zu formulieren und um auszudrücken, dass etwas **höchstwahrscheinlich passiert**, da schon erste Anzeichen dafür vorhanden sind.

  Beispiele: We are going to play tennis tonight.
  I have a temperature. I think I am going to be out of work tomorrow.

- Das ***present progressive*** drückt aus, dass man etwas **fest geplant** hat.

  Beispiel: I am arriving in Berlin tomorrow.

  Eine Zeitangabe, die sich auf die Zukunft bezieht, oder der Zusammenhang müssen deutlich machen, dass es sich um ein Ereignis in der Zukunft handelt, da sonst Verwechslungsgefahr mit dem echten *present progressive* besteht.

- Das ***future progressive*** beschreibt **Ereignisse**, die – geplant oder auch nicht – **sowieso stattfinden** werden. Außerdem bezeichnet es **Handlungen**, die in der **Zukunft ablaufen** werden. Hier ist die **Dauer** betont.

  Beispiele: Even if it rains tomorrow Jim will be training.
  I will be taking part in a workshop next August.

- **Feste Termine** in der Zukunft können im ***simple present*** mitgeteilt werden.

  Beispiel: *Sharon begins work next Tuesday.*

Wie bildest du *future tenses?*

- ***will-future***
  will + Infinitiv des Verbs
  Beispiel: *I/you/he/she/it/we/they <u>will</u> <u>play</u>.*
  Merke: In der **Umgangsprache** wird *I will* oft zu *I'll* und *I will not* zu *I won't.*
- ***going-to-future***
  Form von to be + going to + Infinitiv des Verbs
  Beispiel: I <u>am</u>/you, we, they <u>are</u>/he, she, it <u>is</u> <u>going to</u> <u>play</u>
- ***present progressive***
  siehe S. 44
- ***future progressive***
  will be + *ing*-Form des Verbs
  Beispiel: I/you/he/she/it/we/they <u>will be</u> <u>playing</u>
- ***simple present***
  siehe S. 40

Aufgabe 15* This is the Prime Minister's Diary for tomorrow the 25th of June.

Your task is to write a conversation between a journalist and the P.M.'s Private Secretary asking questions about the Prime Minister's plans for tomorrow. Use words and phrases like what time, how long, what, where, when. Then give answers based on the information above like a Private Secretary might.

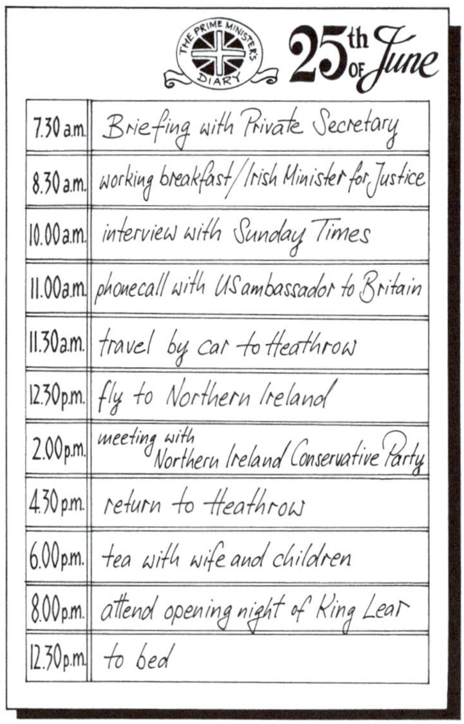

JOURNALIST: Mr Ingham, can I begin by asking you what time the P. M. will be having breakfast?

SECRETARY: Certainly Miss O'Connor. The P. M. will be having a working breakfast with the Irish Minister for Justice at 8.30.

JOURNALIST: How long will breakfast last?

SECRETARY: ______________________________

JOURNALIST: ______________________________

SECRETARY: ______________________________

JOURNALIST: ______________________________

SECRETARY: ______________________________

JOURNALIST: ______________________________

SECRETARY: ______________________________

JOURNALIST: ______________________________

SECRETARY: ______________________________

JOURNALIST: ______________________________

SECRETARY: ______________________________

JOURNALIST: ______________________________

SECRETARY: ______________________________

JOURNALIST: ______________________________

SECRETARY: ______________________________

JOURNALIST: ______________________________

SECRETARY: ______________________________

JOURNALIST: ______________________________

SECRETARY: ______________________________

Aufgabe 16* **Mixed tenses:** State the tense the verbs underlined are in. In each of the examples marked with an asterisk say why this tense is used here.

The old woman brushed her grey hair back with the palm of her hand and sat down at the fire. "When I was a young girl", she said, "I left Liverpool and sailed to America. <u>I had decided</u>* to emigrate and never return. There was no work here for me and <u>I have always been</u> a person who <u>loves</u> to travel. So I <u>left</u> Liverpool in May of 1927 the same month that Charles Lindbergh made the first non-stop solo flight across the Atlantic from New York to Paris. Little <u>did</u>

I know that one day our paths would really cross. I got a job as a house maid in the home of a rich family. They had emigrated from Italy at the turn of the century and were very wealthy. I had lots of work to do but in the evening I was free to do a I pleased. They gave me board and lodging and I was able to save some money. I made friends with a Spanish girl who was working in the house of Charles Lindbergh. Lindbergh, who had just married the daughter of a US politician, was a folk hero all over the world. Lizzy, my friend, used to tell* me all the news and bits of gossip about the Lindberghs and the people who used call to their house. After a while the Lindberghs had a baby, Charles, and once or twice I saw them out walking in the street where we lived. Then, one day, after I had finished my chores, I went to the park where Lizzy and I usually met. She arrived a little later than normal with tears in her eyes. We sat on a bench and she told me how someone had kidnapped the Lindberghs' baby by climbing up a ladder to the nursery on the second floor. The kidnapper had left a ransom note asking for money. The police had been asking Lizzy all sorts of questions during the morning for she, like all the other servants, was under suspicion – She was very upset – "They'll go* out of their minds if anything happens* the child" she said to me. We went for a walk and after she had calmed down I took her to the house where I worked and gave her tea. We sat in the kitchen and talked. In the days that followed she told me everything that was taking place in the house. It was all over the newspapers and the whole of America was talking about the case. After they had paid a lot of money the Lindberghs waited in hope. Then one day I heard that the police had found the baby – dead, somewhere near the Lindbergh home. Shortly afterwards Lizzy lost her job because the Lindberghs decided to emigrate to Europe. That was the worst thing I remember happening in the eight years I spent in New Jersey."

Aufgabe 17 **Irregular verbs:** Derek thinks he has learned his irregular verbs well. The next day he finds the English test his teacher has set him quite difficult. Can you help him? Fill in the missing forms.

a) beat ________ ________

b) bet ________ bet

c) burst ________ burst

d) choose ________ ________

e) draw ________ drawn

f) forbid		forbidden
g) hold		held
h) lay		
i) lie		
j) ride		ridden
k) shake		shaken
l) shrink		
m) swear		
n) teach		taught
o) tear		
p) tell		told
q) throw		
r) wear		worn
s) win		won
t) write		written

Aufgabe 18* Ellis Island II. Translate the following.

Nachdem die Einwanderer die Gespräche und die Gesundheitsuntersuchungen beendet hatten, reisten diese zukünftigen Amerikaner nach New York und in andere Städte weiter. Eine kleine Minderheit kam jedoch schließlich in einen Raum auf Ellis Island, von wo sie zurückgeschickt wurden. Ihre Zukunft hing so sehr von dem ab, was an diesem Tag passierte, dass es für viele ein Erlebnis war, das sie nie vergaßen. Ab 1924, nachdem der Congress ein neues Gesetz verabschiedet hatte, wurde die Insel nicht mehr als Einwanderungslager benutzt.
1990 öffnete Ellis Island wieder, aber diesmal als Museum. Schon Millionen von Amerikanern haben das Zentrum besucht und die ersten Schritte ihrer Vorfahren in der Neuen Welt nachempfunden. Es gab viele andere berühmte Einwanderungslager in der Geschichte der Vereinigten Staaten (Angel Island in San Francisco z. B. wurde ebenfalls berühmt), aber es ist zu bezweifeln, ob auch nur eines von ihnen jemals so bekannt wie Ellis Island werden wird.

Aufgabe 19* Study this advertisement for a Hogmanay Gala. Pretend you have been sent by your newspaper to report on the event. Write a report of all you experienced using as many different tenses as possible.

5 Passiv

Beim **Passiv** *(passive)* wird das **Geschehen betont**. Der Täter, der im Aktiv *(active)* hervorgehoben wird, spielt im Passiv nur eine untergeordnete Rolle.

Beispiel: We keep our money in the bank. *(active)*
Our money is kept in the bank. *(passive)*

5.1 Zeitformen des Passivs

Wann verwendest du das Passiv?

- Du verwendest das Passiv, wenn du nicht weißt, wer etwas getan hat.
  Beispiel: House prices have risen in Vermont.
- Du verwendest das Passiv auch dann, wenn du stärker betonen möchtest was passiert ist, als wer es getan hat.
  Beispiel: The report was presented in time for the shareholders' meeting.

Aus diesen beiden Gründen wird das Passiv in Artikeln, Zeitungsmeldungen, Geschäftsbriefen und in Werbeanzeigen besonders oft benutzt.

Rund um die *simple*-Formen des Passivs

Wie bildest du die *simple*-Formen des Passivs?

Form von *to be* + *past participle*

Beispiel: The company was founded in 2004.

Die folgende Tabelle zeigt dir Aktiv und Passiv in verschiedenen Zeiten der *simple*-Form. Lerne diese Tabelle auswendig!

tense	*active*	*passive*
simple present	He writes poetry.	Poetry is written (by him).
simple past	He wrote poetry.	Poetry was written …
present perfect	He has written poetry.	Poetry has been written …
past perfect	He had written poetry.	Poetry had been written …
future	He will write poetry.	Poetry will be written …
conditional	He would write poetry.	Poetry would be written …
future + conditional	He will/would have written poetry.	Poetry will/would have been written …
gerund	I remember him writing poetry.	I remember poetry being written …
auxiliary + infinitive	He ought to write poetry.	Poetry ought to be written …

Aufgabe 1 **Castle Kilbride:** Underline the passive forms in the following passages and say what tense they are in.

Castle Kilbride in Baden, Canada, was built in 1877 by James Livingston and named after his birthplace in Scotland. Within five years of Livingston's arrival in Baden in 1858, a company had been formed, a flax mill rented, and a linseed oil mill was being constructed. Before long a small fortune had been amassed which allowed him finance the building of Castle McBride.
The Castle's attractive external appearence is overshadowed by its amazing interior decor. To appreciate the artistry in the Castle the visitor will want to see the brilliance of the restored works. The most elaborate paintings are found in the library where scarcely a square inch of wall and ceiling has been left unpainted. The ceiling of the second-floor master bedroom was covered entirely by one huge piece of linen before being painted. The hand painted artwork has been described as one of the finest examples of wall painting in a domestic residence in all of Canada.
Castle Kilbride was purchased by a development company in 1988 after it had been evacuated by the builder's granddaughter. The main basement has been refitted and further restorations are being conducted at present. It is hoped the work will be completed for the forthcoming tourist season.

Aufgabe 2 The early days of the Irish Electricity Supply Board: Your task here is to complete the sentences and by so doing tell the story of the Irish Electricity Supply Board.

In the 19th century electric power (to use) (1) ________________ very little in Ireland. Some years ago the names of the men who first pioneered electricity in Ireland (to place) (2) ________________ on a plaque at Pigeon House in Dublin. In 1918 the idea of harnassing Ireland's water-powered resources (to discuss) (3) ________________ by Theodore Stevens and others. When the Irish Free State (to found) (4) ________________ in 1922 people realized that electricity was vital to industrial progress. Proposals for damming the River Shannon (to submit) (5) ________________ by Dr. Thomas A. McLoghlin. A short time after the proposals (to be accepted) (6) ________________ Siemens-Schuckertwerke of Berlin (to authorize) (7) ________________ by the Irish government to prepare a detailed plan for the building of the first plant at Ardnacrusha near Limerick. While the Shannon scheme (to be constructed) (8) ________________ the E.S.B. Act of 1927 (to pass) (9) ________________ by the Irish government. To meet the needs of Dublin's growing population a project known as the Liffey Scheme (to undertake) (10) ______________ by the E.S.B. between 1937 and 1949. Further schemes (to develop) (11) ______________ and (to complete) (12) ______________ in the years following this.

Aufgabe 3 **Discover the country:** Change the following passage from active to passive voice.

a) In 1494 Christopher Columbus claimed the country for Spain.

____

b) In 1655 the English captured this country from Spain.

____

c) This country grows over two hundred native species of orchids.

____

d) Shortly after the Second World War the people cast their votes for the first time.

____

e) The inhabitants of this country speak English and a dialect called patois.

____

f) The women wear a traditional dress consisting of a long skirt and a head-dress made out of bandana.

____

g) To earn a living the people farm the land.

____

h) However, they also cater for the many tourists who come every year.

____

i) In 1720, Nanny of the Maroons led the people in a war against the British.

____

j) Sprinter Merlene Ottey ran world fastest times for the 100 and 200 metres in the 1980s and 1990s.

____

The name of this country is ______________________

Aufgabe 4* The following changes have all been made by the new owners of Arklow Manor. Describe what repairs have been carried out. Use these verbs: *to rebuild, to put in, to re-hang, to erect, to fix, to make, to insert, to plant, to tidy up, to buy.*

a) The chimney *has been rebuilt by the new owners.*

b) A new kitchen window ______

c) The front door ______

d) A brand new fence ______

e) The hole in the roof ______

f) Attractive new curtains ______

g) A sky-light ______

h) New trees ______

i) The garden ______

j) A new drainpipe ______

Aufgabe 5 **Thanksgiving:** Change these to the passive. In nearly all cases you have to use some form of a future or conditional tense. You should start your first two answers with the underlined words.

a) Americans would normally start <u>preparations for Thanksgiving</u> days beforehand.

b) You will find <u>differences in the Thanksgiving menu</u> from family to family.

c) A Thanksgiving shopping list would include sweet potatoes, onions, green peas, cranberry sauce, nuts, fruit and candies.

d) Usually, the person preparing the feast will bake pies.

e) Families would also buy or make greeting cards.

f) All Americans would see the turkey as the centrepiece of the meal.

g) The cook will, of course, fill the great bird with all sorts of delicious stuffing.

h) Americans will reserve a special place for the turkey on the Thanksgiving dinner table for years to come.

i) The parents will have put in a lot of work by the time the feast comes round.

j) At the first Pilgrims' Thanksgiving feast the people would have eaten wild turkey roasted over an open fire.

k) They would also have enjoyed fish and venison.

l) The first pilgrims would have found corn buried in sand.

m) A family celebrating Thanksgiving will often hang up ears of corn as decorations.

n) Many people will eat pumpkins as a dessert next Thanksgiving because it is said the original pilgrims ate pumpkins.

Rund um die *progressive*-Formen des Passivs

Wie bildest du die *progressive*-Formen des Passivs?

Form von *to be* + *being* + *past participle*

Beispiel: The car was being repaired by my mother.

Die folgende Tabelle zeigt dir Aktiv und Passiv im *present* und im *past tense* der *progressive*-Form. Lerne auch diese Tabelle auswendig!

tense	*active*	*passive*
present progressive	She is reading a book.	A book is being read by her.
past progressive	She was reading a book.	A book was being read by her.

Aufgabe 6 Study the following cartoon. Then describe what is happening in the present tense progressive, active and passive!

a) (to hang up the washing)

The woman is hanging up the washing.

The washing is being hung up by the woman.

b) (to bake a cake)

c) (to water the plants)

d) (to use the hoover)

e) (to read the paper)

f) (to ask a question)

g) (to make a phonecall)

h) (to smoke a cigarette)

i) (to do absolutely nothing)

j) (to do all the jobs)

5.2 Passiv und das Objekt des Satzes

Rund um Verben mit direktem und indirektem Objekt

Wenn du einen Aktivsatz, der sowohl ein direktes als auch ein indirektes Objekt *(direct, indirect object)* hat, ins Passiv umwandelst, können beide Objekte Subjekt des Passivsatzes werden.

Beispiel:	Tom's mother bought him a football shirt yesterday.	*(active)*
	A football shirt was bought by Tom's mother yesterday.	*(passive)*
	Tom was bought a football shirt by his mother yesterday.	*(passive)*

Folgende Verben haben oft zwei Objekte nach sich: *to allow, to appoint, to ask, to call, to deny, to give, to hand, to leave, to offer, to order, to pay, to sell, to tell.*

Aufgabe 7 **Will Rogers** – One of America's most famous cowboys.

The American cowboy Will Rogers was one of the country's most famous Wild West characters. In this exercise you have to form two passive sentences from each of the following pieces of information about Will Rogers. One passive sentence should have the direct object, the other the indirect object, as its subject. Look carefully at the example before you begin.

a) Will Rogers bought his children a newspaper nearly everyday.
A newspaper was bought by Will Rogers for his children nearly every day.
Will Rogers' children were bought a newspaper nearly every day.

b) An American cattle farmer gave the young Will Rogers a job as a cattle hand.

c) Soon the owner of a Wild West show offered him a position as an entertainer.

d) The man promised Will more money if he was good.

e) Will often taught the visitors simple rope tricks.

f) Will also told the people good jokes that he had read in newspapers.

g) In 1908 Will bought his girl Betty a wedding ring.

h) He promised her a good and happy life.

i) When he died in 1935 America gave Will Rogers a fitting funeral.

Rund um das Passiv bei Verben mit präpositionalem Objekt

Wenn du einen Aktivsatz mit einem präpositionalen Objekt *(prepositional object)* in einen Passivsatz umwandelst, darfst du auch **im Passivsatz die Präposition nicht vom Verb trennen**.

Beispiel: We sent for the vet. *(active)*
The vet was sent for. *(passive)*

Lerne die folgenden Verben mit ihren Präpositionen auswendig:

to agree on:	sich einigen auf
to apologize for:	sich entschuldigen für
to arrive at:	(an)kommen
to ask for:	bitten um
to complain of:	sich beklagen über
to deal with:	etwas behandeln
to dream of:	träumen von
to feel sorry for:	Leid tun
to get angry at:	ärgerlich sein über
to hear of:	hören von
to listen to:	zuhören
to learn from:	ersehen aus
to look at:	anschauen
to look after:	sich um etwas kümmern
to laugh at:	lachen über
to pay for:	zahlen für
to rely on:	sich verlassen auf
to send for:	schicken nach
to think of:	denken über

Aufgabe 8 Put the following into the passive voice.

In the 1950s the people of the Blasket Islands, a group of islands off the west coast of Ireland, arrived at an important decision. They agreed to a government proposal to leave the islands and accept land on the mainland in return. They had thought about the proposals carefully beforehand. The islanders spoke

Irish and relied upon land and sea to stay alive. After the Great War the numbers of fish the people were catching grew smaller. They now relied on financial support from sons and daughters in America to stay alive. Every winter they dealt with the poverty of their hard lives as best they could. They heard about the resettlement proposals and discussed them. One or two islanders laughed at the idea at first. Most of the people however listened to the proposals. They asked the government for help. Eventually, in 1953, officials took the people off the island.

Nützliche Passiv-Konstruktionen

Einige Verben werden am Satzanfang besonders gerne im Passiv verwendet. Diese Verben können vor allem beim Schreiben eines Aufsatzes gut eingesetzt werden.

Beispiel: It is (often) said …

Am besten lernst du diese Verben auswendig: *to accept, to agree, to hope, to expect, to say, to remember, to decide, to assume, to think, to believe, to acknowledge, to understand, to claim, to know, to regret, to take for granted.*

Aufgabe 9 First of all learn these by heart and then complete them by finishing the sentence. Each sentence should be about an MP who is about to resign.

a) It is more or less agreed that the M.P. should resign.

b) It is generally believed that ____________

c) It is widely hoped that ____________

d) It has been decided that ____________

e) It is fully accepted that ____________

f) It is to be regretted that ____________

g) It must be remembered that ____________

h) It has often been said that ____________

i) It is (frequently) taken for granted that ____________

j) It is thought that ____________

Aufgabe 10* Write a comment using as many of the passive phrases from exercise 9 as you can plus other examples of passive constructions!

A European motorway Speed Limit of 120 km per hour would be a good thing ...

Aufgabe 11* **Revision:** It is 2004 and you are busy writing a book called *A Guide to the Museums of Britain and Ireland.* You visit the National Army Museum in London. Later when you come to write a description of the location, history, contents and opening hours of the museum you find the following written in your note-book:

Memo

- Location: Royal Hospital Road, Chelsea, London
- History: established 1960
  since 1960: Museum has collected/exhibited materials relating to the British Army
- Contents: 2 galleries devoted to chronological survey of Army (1485-1982).
  Uniform Gallery houses weapons,medals and insignia.
  Art Gallery contains 17th, 18th, 19th century paintings.
  The Weapon Gallery traces development of hand weapons.
- Send enquiries to The Curator, National Army Museum, Royal Hospital Road, Chelsea, London SW3 4HT
- Contact Mr Bottomley for group tours: Tel 0171 730 0717
- When may you visit the museum?:
  Mon-Sat 10.00-5.30
  Sun 2.00-5.30
- Other interesting info:
  building a new wing at the moment
  2004: they hope to carry out further extensions
- The Duke of Wellington would really have appreciated this museum!

Now take the above notes and write a brief guide to the museum. Your account should be mainly in the passive voice.

The National Army Museum is located in Chelsea, London.

6 Modale Hilfsverben

Hilfsverben (*auxiliaries*) können – im Gegensatz zu Vollverben – nicht alleine stehen, sondern immer nur zusammen mit einem anderen Verb (daher auch der Name „Hilfsverb"). Mit den **modalen Hilfsverben** kannst du ganz bestimmte **Sprechabsichten** ausdrücken.

Hilfsverben unterscheiden sich von Vollverben in einer Reihe von Punkten:

- Hilfsverben haben **keine Infinitiv-** und **keine Partizip-Form**.
- In der **3. Person Singular** stehen Hilfsverben **ohne -*s***.
  Beispiel: Terry can play chess.
- In **Fragen** und **Verneinungen** stehen Hilfsverben **ohne *to do***.
  Beispiele: Can you play chess?
  I can't play chess!
- Hilfsverben können nicht in alle Zeiten gesetzt werden. In den Zeiten, in denen Hilfsverben nicht gebraucht werden können, z. B. im Futur, musst du **Ersatzformen** verwenden.
  Beispiel: David will have to train harder.

6.1 *may/might*

Wann verwendest du *may/might?*

Du verwendest *may/might*, um folgende Dinge auszudrücken:

- **Erlaubnis**, etwas zu tun
  Beispiel: You may turn over your exam papers.
- **Wahrscheinlichkeit** bzw. **Unwahrscheinlichkeit**
  Beispiel: It might be a good idea to switch the machine on.

Die **Ersatzform** von *may/might* lautet *to be allowed to.*

Aufgabe 1 Imagine you find yourself in the situations described below. What would you say? Each answer should contain may or might.

a) You're off to a new country and afraid it won't work out.
It might not work out.

b) You'd like to borrow someone's pen.

c) You're in a train and it's too hot.

d) You doing a driving test tomorrow and are afraid you will fail.

____

e) You want a visa for a holiday but don't know if you'll get it.

____

f) You want the butter, which is at the other end of the table.

____

g) You need information at a trade fair and go to enquiries.

____

h) You want to turn up the radio but there are other people in the room.

____

6.2 *must, must not / need not*

Wann verwendest du *must, must not / need not?*

- Du verwendest ***must***, wenn du ausdrücken möchtest, dass jemand etwas **zu machen hat** und wenn du bestimmte **Schlüsse ziehst**.
  Ersatzform: *to have to*
  Beispiele: I must go to the doctor. I feel ill.
  That must be Tom's hat. He left it here last week.
- ***mustn't*** verwendest du, um ein **Verbot** auszudrücken.
  Ersatzform: *not to have to*
  Beispiel: You mustn't cross the road when the light is red.
- ***needn't*** gebrauchtst du, wenn du jemandem sagen willst, was **nicht getan werden** muss.
  Beispiel: You needn't do your work until after tea.

Aufgabe 2 How would you react if someone said the following to you? Use *must, mustn't, needn't* etc.

a) The flowers are dying in the heat.
I must water them then.

b) The baby is crying. He ______________ be hungry. I'll feed him.
No, you ______________ feed him, he ______________ to be changed.

c) You got a parking ticket two weeks ago.
I ______________ park on a yellow line again.

d) Your fingernails are too long.
I __________ them then!

e) The sittingroom is in an awful state.
You __________ clean it today, tomorrow will do.

f) How fast may I drive on Irish motorways?
You __________ than 70 mph.

g) I can't read the signs with these old glasses of mine.
__________ then!

h) I've put on 12 kilos in the last year.
____

Aufgabe 3 John and his mother are talking at home. Complete the following sentences with the correct word to find out what they are saying: *may, must, mustn't, needn't.*

JOHN: ________ I do my homework right now Mam? ________ I watch TV instead?

MOTHER: You ________ if you don't want to. You ________ do it later if you like. But you ________ have it done before your brothers come home. Sit back from the TV. You know you ________ sit too close to the TV. The doctor said it's bad for your eyes. And don't put your feet on the arm of the sofa. How many times have I said you ________ do that. I ________ be talking to myself again. I've told you that a thousand times. Do you ever listen?

JOHN: Why ______ children do everything their parents tell them? It's not fair.

MOTHER: When you're a father yourself it will be better. Then you ________ do anything except what your wife tells you!

JOHN: I ________ remember that! Oh! ________ I have an icecream?

MOTHER: Before your tea! You ________ not.

6.3 *shall/should, ought to*

Wann verwendest du *shall/should, ought to?*

- Du verwendest ***shall/should***, wenn du einen **Vorschlag** oder ein **Angebot** machen möchtest.
  Ersatzform: *to be to*
  Beispiele: Shall I draw the bird?
  Should you need more tea or coffee please let me know.
- ***should/ought to*** kannst du gebrauchen, wenn du eine **Verpflichtung** oder einen **Ratschlag** ausdrücken möchtest.
  Beispiele: You should spend more time at your homework.
  You ought to quit smoking.

Aufgabe 4 What offers of advice or help would you make to the following people? Use *shall* or *should* in your answer.

a) 

You should eat more! ____________________

b) 

____

c) 

____

d) 

e) 

f) 

g) 

Für das deutsche Wort ‚sollen' gibt es verschiedene **Übersetzungsmöglichkeiten**, je nachdem, in welchem Zusammenhang du es verwenden möchtest:

• Soll ich die Arbeit machen?	Shall/Will I do the work?
• Sie sollen jetzt zu Tom kommen.	You are to come to Tom now.
• Der Bus soll eine Verspätung haben.	The bus is said to be late.
• Du solltest ihm mehr Freiheit geben.	You should give him more freedom.
• Du solltest nicht so viel Bier trinken.	You oughtn't to drink so much beer.

Aufgabe 5 Translation I

a) Soll ich Anita etwas schenken?

____

b) Solche Gehälter sollten nicht erlaubt sein.

____

c) Sie sollte lieber bleiben.

____

d) Jane sollte das Auto nicht zu billig verkaufen.

____

e) Mein Vater hätte ihr das Auto nicht schenken sollen.

____

f) Jim soll sein Haus verkauft haben.

____

g) Die Lieferung soll sehr schnell ausgeführt werden.

____

h) Du sollst sofort das Wohnzimmer aufräumen.

____

6.4 *can / could*

Wann verwendest du *can / could?*

- Du verwendest ***can/could***, um eine **Fähigkeit**, eine **Erlaubnis** und eine **Möglichkeit** auszudrücken.
  Ersatzform: *to be able to*
  Beispiele: Susy can do the work when she comes home.
  The students can smoke in the smoking room.
  Do you think you could get him to play?
- ***could*** kann *past tense* von *can* sein. Mit *could* kannst du aber auch sagen, dass etwas **vielleicht passieren wird**. Außerdem kannst du *could* in besonders **höflichen Fragen** benutzen.
  Beispiele: I couldn't work last Friday
  They could arrive tonight.
  Could you pass me the butter please?

Aufgabe 6 Form sentences.

a) Simon can play basketball.
When Simon was in school he could play basketball.
When he finishes university he will still be able to play basketball.

b) Don can speak English.
When he was two years old ______
If he loses his voice ______

c) The girls can ski very well.
When they were young ______
When they are old and grey ______

d) Mags can't swim.
When she lived in Canada she ______ either.
After she has lived in Spain for a while ______

Aufgabe 7 **When I was your age:** In this exercise you must imagine you are talking to a person, Nora, who was born at the turn of the century when things were different. Write a full sentence for each of you based on the information given.

a) (may) to go on holiday

You: My parents have said I may go on holidays with my friends in the summer.

Nora: I wasn't allowed to go on holidays with my friends. My family was too poor.

b) (must) to study hard if I want to pass my exams

You: My parents have said

Nora: ______

c) (can) to do my driving test at the age of eighteen

You: ______

Nora: ______

d) (must) to dispose of our rubbish carefully

You: ______

Nora: ______

e) My parents say I (may/to go) to a disco once a week

You: ______

Nora: ______

f) (can) to fly to any part of the world

You: ______

Nora: ______

g) (must) to get a job and start a career after school

You: ______

Nora: ______

Aufgabe 8 **A Shepherd and his sheep:** In the following exercise your task is to change these sentences into the negative form.

a) The shepherd must look after his sheep.
______________________________ after they have been sold.

b) Yesterday he had to tend to a limping ewe's sore foot.
Last week ______________________________

c) Next year the shepherd will have a new lot of sheep to care for.
Tomorrow ______________________________

d) Yesterday the shepherd's dog had to work hard.
Last night ______________________________

e) The dog needs to run quickly in order to catch the sheep.
______________________________ when the sheep are tired.

f) The shepherd can whistle very well.
He ______________________________ when he's hoarse.

g) The shepherd must take shelter during thunderstorms.
______________________________ from a light shower.

Aufgabe 9 **Revision:** The following sentences are all based on the cartoon. Fill in the blanks using the necessary modal auxiliary.

O·brien

a) The woman ______________ barely lift the crate of beer.

b) She ______________ have a sore back after carrying the crate into the room.

c) Her husband ______________ drink enormous amounts of beer.

d) If she had wanted a more enjoyable evening she ________________ have spent the evening with friends.

e) The cat which is fast asleep on the sofa ________________ be drunk.

f) This woman will ________________ find herself a new husband if she wants a better life.

g) For the sake of his health this man ________________ stop drinking.

h) The woman ________________ like to have a drink herself if she had the time.

i) Who do you think ________________ clear up the bottles at the end of the evening?

j) This man ________________ worry about that – he looks as if he will fall asleep soon!

Aufgabe 10 **Revision:** Your task here is to translate the following statements into English.

a) Sie sollten sich dafür schämen.

____

b) Sie muss die Dinge akzeptieren, wie sie sind und das Beste daraus machen.

____

c) Und wir sollen und wir können und wir dürfen keine weiteren 8 Monate warten, bis wir ein Gesetz bekommen.

____

d) Sollte ich der Demokratischen Partei beitreten?

____

e) Sie sollte den Bibelverkäufer um 10 Uhr treffen.

____

f) Ich muss ein Telegramm nach Portland schicken.

____

g) Wir hätten Tom nicht nach Chicago schicken sollen.

____

h) Dad sagte, er musste das auch tun, als er klein war.

____

7 Infinitiv

Der **Infinitiv** (*infinitiv*) ist die **Grundform des Verbs**. Er gehört zu den **infiniten Verbformen** und enthält daher keine Informationen zur grammatischen Person und zur Zahl. Der Infinitv kann **mit *to***, aber auch **ohne *to*** stehen und er kann von allen Verben, ausgenommen den modalen Hilfsverben, gebildet werden. Es gibt sowohl **Aktiv-** als auch **Passiv-Formen** des Infinitivs.

Beispiele:

Mit *to*

Tony wants to bake a cake. (Aktiv)
The car ought to be repaired. (Passiv)

Ohne *to*

Tony may bake a cake later. (Aktiv)
The car must be repaired today. (Passiv)

7.1 Infinitv mit *to*

Viele Vollverben ziehen den Infinitv mit *to* nach sich. Er kommt aber auch sehr oft in festen grammatischen Konstruktionen vor.

Rund um verschiedene grammatische Konstruktionen

Wann verwendest du die Konstruktion: Verb + Infinitiv?

Auf manche Verben folgt der Infinitiv. Die wichtigsten sind hier aufgelistet. Lerne sie auswendig!

to agree	Do you agree to pay him 100 pounds?
to afford	I can't afford to pay that much.
to appear	He appears to be in a spot of bother.
to ask	I asked to see the priest.
to attempt	They will attempt to free him tomorrow.

to arrange, to bother (negative), to care (negative), to choose, to consent, to decide, to expect, to fail, to forget, to guarantee, to happen, to hesitate, to hope, to learn, to manage, to neglect, to plan, to pretend, to promise, to refuse, to seem, to tend, to try, to volunteer, to wish

Aufgabe 1 **Vocabulary exercise:** The following words are to be found in the next story. Consult a dictionary and explain them in your own words.

a) to rouse ______________________

b) to regret ______________________

c) horrid ______________________

d) from scratch ______________________

e) hasty ______________________

Aufgabe 2 The History of Dr Jekyll and Mr Hyde: In this exercise you have to complete the sentence with a suitable infinitive. You also have to decide whether the tale is a true or false one!
The infinitives to be used at some stage in the story are: *to finish, to read, to like, to rouse, to listen, to regret, to argue, to publish, to throw, to rescue, to work, to wake, to dream, to show*

A WINTER'S NIGHT, 1885: The writer, R. L. Stevenson begins (1) __________ in his sleep.

ONE HOUR LATER: Frightened by his screams of terror, his wife Fanny decides (2) __________ her husband.

SHORTLY AFTER THAT: After she manages (3) __________ him he gives out to her for disturbing his sleep!

NEXT MORNING: Stevenson sets (4) __________ on a new book.

NEXT TWO DAYS: The writer attempts (5) __________ the book as fast as he can. He promises (6) __________ the book to his wife when it's finished.

FOURTH DAY: Stevenson agrees (7) __________ the book to Fanny.

AFTER A WHILE: Fanny refuses (8) __________ to any more of the horrid tale and starts (9) __________ with Stevenson. They have a terrible row! His wife threatens (10) __________ the book into the fire! Stevenson tries (11) ______________ the manuscript from her, succeeds, and becomes so angry that he flings it into the fire himself!

DAYS 5–7: Stevenson seems (12) __________________ his hasty action because he sits down and rewrites the 30,000 words from scratch again!

DAY 8: This time Fanny appears (13) ____________ the book a lot more because they do not quarrel and seem happy.

1886: Stevenson plans (14) __________________ the book with a well-known publisher and the book appears later in the year.

I believe this story to be a) true ☐ b) false ☐

Wann verwendest du die Konstruktion: Verb + Objekt + Infinitv?

Verben, die einen **Wunsch**, ein **Vorhaben**, eine **Meinung**, eine **Warnung**, einen **Tipp** formulieren ziehen häufig den Infinitv mit to nach sich. Darunter die Folgenden: *want, tell, advise, note, ask, expect, help, mean, prefer, wish, love.* Sie stehen dabei oft in der Verbindung Verb + Objekt + Infinitv.

Beispiel: I invited him to accompany me to the dance.
(invited = Verb, him = Objekt, to accompany = Infinitiv mit to)

Aufgabe 3 Listening to Dad! Barry's Dad means well but he is always telling him what to do. Sometimes he does that nicely, sometimes not so nicely. Your task is to match the verbs *want, ask, expect, tell, advise, encourage, order* and *beg* to the various things his Dad says.

a) Barry's Dad told him to clean up his room.

b) __________

c) __________

d) __________

e) __________

f) __________

g) __________

h) __________

Aufgabe 4 The following pictures describe some moments in the story of Nelson Mandela's life. Your task is to build full sentences from the words and pictures.

a)

(to force himself/ at university)

I forced myself to study hard at university.

b)

(to persuade)

I persuaded a man …

c)

(to ask)

In 1957 …

d)

(to use/ Rivonia Trial)

e)

(to encourage/ supporters)

f)

(to warn/Botha)

g)

(to invite/Botha)

---

h)

(to help)

---

i)

(to write)

---

j)

(to visit)

Rund um die Funktionen des Infinitivs im Satz

Wie kannst du den Infinitiv im Satz einsetzen?

- Da der Infinitiv als infinite Verbform Eigenschaften von Verben, aber auch Eigenschaften von Nomen besitzt, kannst du ihn als **Subjekt eines Satzes** verwenden.
  Beispiel: To drive under the influence of drink is a criminal act.
- Zur Verkürzung von Sätzen kannst du den Infinitv mit *to* auch **anstelle eines Relativsatzes** verwenden.
  Beispiel: Cavan is the place where you can buy beautiful glass.
  Cavan is the place to buy beautiful glass.
- Ebenfalls zur Satzverkürzung kannst in **indirekten Fragesätzen** den Infinitiv zur **Auflösung des Nebensatzes** einsetzen.
  Beispiel: Don't you know where you should go?
  Don't you know where to go?
- Nach **Ordnungszahlen** und ***the first, the last, the only*** kannst du ebenfalls den Infinitiv mit *to* verwenden.
  Beispiele: I am the first member of my family to become a doctor.
  She was the only one to pass the exam.

Aufgabe 5 **Mixed exercise:** Before you try this translation make sure you've read the last three grammatical points. Translate into English:

a) Eileen war das erste Mädchen, das zur Vorlesung erschien.

____

b) Der Inspektor war der einzige Mensch, der mir zu Hilfe kam.

____

c) Weißt du denn nicht, wie man eine Schleife bindet?

____

d) Der Premierminister war der letzte, der das Flugzeug bestieg.

____

Aufgabe 6 **Mixed exercise:** What to do in Kerry!

You live in County Kerry in Ireland. Study the ads and complete the sentences in line with the examples given. For the answers try using other phrases *like the first, the last,* as well as *the only*.

a) O'Mahony's
- To order educational supplies you should go to O'Mahony's.
- O'Mahony's is the only shop in Kerry to sell good books.
- O'Mahony's is the place to buy play equipment.

b) John Crean (Speedy Cabs)
-
-
- John Crean is the man …

c) Ahern's Garage
-
-
-

d) Lyons Antiques
-
-
-

e) Barry Print and Packaging
-
-
-

f) Dan Fitzgerald
-
-
-

g) Hugh Culloty
-
-
-

h) Páidí Ó Sé's Pub in Ventry
-
-
-

Now take the third sentence of each of your answers and rewrite it using a relative clause.

i) O'Mahony's is the place where one/you can buy play equipment.

j) ______

k) ______

l) ______

m) ______

n) ______

o) ______

p) ______

Aufgabe 7 Why would you become ...? Study the example and complete the list.

a) (a doctor) Why would you become a doctor?
I would become a doctor to cure the sick.

b) (a sailor) ______

c) (a vet) ______

d) (a writer) ______

e) (a pilot) ______

f) (a postman) ______

g) (a newsreader) ______

h) (a trade union official) ______

7.2 Infinitiv ohne *to*

Wann verwendest du den Infinitiv ohne *to*?

- Du verwendest den Infinitiv ohne *to* **nach allen modalen Hilfsverben** mit Ausnahme von *ought* und nach *need* und *dare*, wenn diese als Hilfsverben verwendet werden.

  Beispiele: You must not give out to him like that.
  You needn't bring cutlery.
  I daren't give out to him.
  aber: You ought to mind your records better.

- Nach **Verben des Wahrnehmens und des Beobachtens** verwendest du den Infinitiv ohne *to*.

  Beispiel: I saw Tom take the bus.

- Nach ***make*** (im Sinne von ‚lassen') und nach ***let*** gebrauchst du den Infinitiv ohne *to*.

  Beispiele: His mother makes him cut the grass.
  Ian let us have his boathouse all summer.

- Nach Wendungen wie ***… had better, … would rather, … would sooner*** etc. folgt der Infinitiv ohne *to*.

  Beispiel: I had better take the train.

Aufageb 8 To? With or without – Complete the following story by inserting the infinitive. You must decide whether it is the form in brackets that is needed or simply the infinite without to.

"Shall I (to tell) (1) ________________ you a strange tale" my piano teacher said to me one day, as we came to the end of another lesson. I smiled and, knowing how long Herr Gabler's stories could be, simply said "it had better (to be) (2) ________________ a fairly short one. My mother's waiting outside". "You ought (to forget) (3) ________________ about your mother and (to listen) (4) ________________ more to your old piano teacher," he laughed. "I see her (to drive) (5) ________________ off to work every morning and she never has the time (to say) (6) ________________ hello to the man who teaches her son the fine art of the piano! Anyhow, I'll be brief. The Italian-born composer Jean Babtiste Lully had one of the strangest musical deaths of all time. Director of music at the court of Louis XIV, he was a fantastic conductor and made everyone (to work) (7) ________________ extremely hard. In 1687 he decided he would rather (to conduct) (8) ________________ *Te Deum* than any other piece. In the course of the performance he accidentally struck himself on the foot with the heavy staff which he was using to show the musicians the correct tempo.

His fellow musicians stood up (to make) (9) ______________ room so that the injured Lully could (to be) (10) ____________ treated. '(To let) (11) ____________ him bleed to death' is the comment one nasty rival of Bully's is said to have muttered. Lully overheard the comment and replied 'I would sooner (to roast) (12) ______________ in hell than (to give) (13) ______________ you the pleasure of seeing me (to die) (14) ______________ in the course of a performance'. Unfortunately for Lully the wound was allowed (to go) (15) ______________ septic and gangrene set in. Lully's friends watched him (to die) (16) ______________ at the age of 54."

Aufgabe 9* **Revision:** Practice makes perfect! For this training exercise in school tests you will need someone who is able to read English. Perhaps your mother or father will be able to read the dictation to you. Many of the difficult words in this dictation have already turned up in the chapters previous to this. The rest you do on your own. Time allowed: 30 minutes.

a) Dictation

After he had finished his chores Martin Smith sauntered indoors and turned on the television. The flat was totally empty and he settled down to enjoy a film. At that precise moment he heard a noise in the hall and went out to see what it was. His brother Kevin was just arriving home. He had been down at the Labour Exchange trying to find a job. He didn't have much of a chance of finding one because he had no training and very few skills. All he could do was play football but so far no club had showed any serious interest in him. "Hi kid" Kevin yelled into the sitting-room without waiting for a reply. Kevin threw himself lazily on to the couch, grabbed the remote control and switched over to BBC 1 where a furious, nailbiting top-of-the-table soccer match was coming to a dramatic conclusion. "Hey that's not fair", Martin cried, but his brother wasn't listening. "You're a right spoilsport. I wanted to watch the James Bond film." "Be a good lad and do your homework kid" his brother retorted. Martin slammed the door behind him and headed for his bedroom in the attic of the tenement house his family lived in. It was sometimes rotten having a big brother!

b) Grammar

Change the following sentences by using the infinitive! Then write down the name of the person in question.

- This well-known tennis player was not the first American who won the US Open.
- But she was the first person who had followed the difficult road from her native home in a poor eastern European country to incredible fame and fortune in the tennis world.
- In the many finals she played in, this famous tennis star knew what she should do if an opponent tried to psyche her out.
- Besides, she had enormous reserves of strength which she could call on to help her out of a tight corner.
- Her greatest achievement was that she won Wimbledon nine times.

Name of person: ______________________________

c) Creative writing

Write a short paragraph on what it would be like to be the first female head of a secondary school.

8 Gerundium

Auch das **Gerundium** *(gerund)* zählt zu den **infiniten Verbformen**, denn es enthält – genau wie der Infinitiv und das Partizip – keine Angaben zur grammatischen Person, zur Zahl und zur Zeit. Die *ing*-Form – so wird das Gerundium auch oft genannt – kann sowohl im Aktiv als auch im Passiv stehen und von jedem englischen Vollverb gebildet werden. Die Bildung der *ing*-Form kannst du noch einmal auf Seite 44 wiederholen.

Wann verwendest du das Gerundium?

Weil das Gerundium sowohl **Eigenschaften eines Verbs als auch die eines Nomens** besitzt, kannst du das Gerundium in folgenden Situationen verwenden:

- als **Subjekt oder Teil eines Subjekts**

  Beispiele: Learning languages takes time.
  The making of 'Ryan's Daughter' took a long time.

- als **Objekt** eines Satzes

  Beispiel: They both loved reading.

Aufgabe 1

The following sentences describe Susan Mulligan's attitudes to the monthly telephone bill. Your job is to change the sentences introducing a gerund form.

a) It is not very nice to get our monthly telephone bill.

Getting our telephone bill is not very nice.

b) It gives me a horrible feeling to open the envelope and take out the bill.

____

c) It is very costly to have a telephone, a husband, two sons and two daughters!

____

d) It is difficult to make a phonecall in my house.

____

e) It is unpleasant to see my bank statement after my bill has been paid.

____

f) It is stupid to worry about the matter.

____

g) It is much better to have a chat with my neighbour, Ann Dunne.

____

h) It makes me feel good to hear the size of her telephone bill!

____

She has a husband, three daughters and three sons!

Aufgabe 2 The gerund as subject/object of the sentence: In the following exercise you have to match the gerunds with the correct sentence endings.

(1) Swimming ...	(A) ... because the game was sold out.
(2) Catching a cold ...	(B) ... because of the health risk involved
(3) Getting tickets was difficult ...	(C) ... must be hard to organize
(4) Tom likes drinking wine ...	(D) ... can be bad for your health.
(5) Getting married ...	(E) ... is a total waste of time.
(6) Watching football ...	(F) ... is easier than speaking it.
(7) Smoking is dangerous ...	(G) ... is good for your arm muscles.
(8) Sitting down all day ...	(H) ... is a big step in life.
(9) Climbing mountains ...	(I) ... starts with a sneeze.
(10) Many boys hate dancing ...	(J) ... is an outdoor pastime.
(11) She stopped teaching ...	(K) ... when he goes out to dinner.
(12) Reading English ...	(L) ... weeks before her son was born.
(13) Obtaining a loan that size ...	(M) ... because they're self-conscious.

- **nach manchen Verben mit Präposition**

Beispiel: I have often thought of travelling to Austria.

Lerne die folgenden Verben und ihre Präposition, nach denen immer das Gerundium steht, auswendig:

to agree on:	sich einigen auf
to apologize for:	sich entschuldigen für
to complain of:	sich beklagen über
to despair of:	verzweifeln an
to depend on:	abhängen von
to dream of:	träumen von
to look forward to:	sich freuen auf
to succeed in:	gelingen
to rely on:	sich verlassen auf
to think of:	denken über
to insist on:	bestehen auf
to object to:	einwenden gegen
to worry about:	sich Sorgen machen

- **nach manchen Adjektiven mit Präposition**

Beispiel: Michael is good at working with children.

Lerne die folgenden Adjektive und ihre Präposition, nach denen oft das Gerundium steht, auswendig:

to be afraid of:	fürchten, dass
to be crazy about:	verrückt sein nach
to be clever at:	geschickt sein in
to be famous for:	berühmt sein für
to be fond of:	etwas gern tun
to be proud of:	stolz sein auf
to be tired of:	satt haben
to be sorry about:	Leid tun, dass
to be worried about:	sich sorgen über

to be keen on → verrückt sein auf → begeistert sein von
to be excited about
to be interested in
to be ashamed of

Aufgabe 3 **The Story of Hockey:** How much do you know about the history of ice-hockey? In this exercise you should fill in the missing prepositions and gerunds to complete the story of ice-hockey.

Montreal has always been proud of (to be) (1) ___being___ the home of ice-hockey. Most hockey fans there know that the name J. G. A. Creighton will always be famous (2) ___for___ (to help) (3) ___helping___ invent the game of hockey. As a student at McGill University Creighton met other sportsmen who played rugby. Creighton was keen (4) ___on___ (to find) (5) ___finding___ new sports to play. He and his new friends came up with hockey. On March 3, 1875, The Gazette, a Montreal newspaper, announced that a "Hockey" game

would be played that evening at the Victoria Skating rink. 40 people attended that first game. Nearly all of them were excited (6) _____ (to witness) (7) _____ such a momentous event. One person however wrote to the Gazette to complain (8) _____ (not/to be) (9) _____ able to skate. He said he was worried (10) _____ (to have) (11) _____ the rink taken away from skaters. To make matters worse he didn't find the game interesting. He said he soon got tired (12) _____ (to watch) (13) _____ it and went home. In 1883 the first tournament took place in Montreal. The year after people interested (14) _____ (to spread) (15) _____ the game set up the first hockey league. In Montreal of course. By the 1930s Hockey had shown everybody that they shouldn't be ashamed (16) _____ (to play) (17) _____ a mixture of rugby, lacrosse, hurling, shinty and bandy while skating on ice! The League even had its own superstar in Howie Morenz (1902–1937). Today many young Canadians dream (18) _____ (to win) (19) _____ the Stanley Cup, hockey's most prized possession.

- **nach manchen Nomen mit Präposition**

Beispiel: They had no hope of getting there on time.

Lerne auch die folgende Liste auswendig:

advantage of:	Vorteil (von)
danger of:	Gefahr zu
habit of:	gewohnt sein, etwas zu tun
objection to:	Einwand gegen
opportunity of:	Gelegenheit haben, etwas zu tun
pleasure in:	Vergnügen haben
reason for:	Grund für
trouble in:	Schwierigkeit

Aufgabe 4 **Hockey:** Part Two. Fill in the blanks with prepositions and gerunds as you think correct.

For many of the founders of the game of hockey the great advantage (1) __of__ (to play) (2) ________ hockey was that it is suited to ice (3) ________ a way other sports aren't. The winter in Montreal is long and cold and before hockey was invented people had tried to play the summer game of lacrosse on ice (4) ________ winter. The danger (5) ________ (to try) (6) ________ to play lacrosse on ice was that without the support of a stick the players kept falling. Players were in the habit (7) ________ (to hit) (8) ________ each other on the head and they took little pleasure (9) ________ (to partake) (10) ________ in a sport in which they kept falling over. So once the opportunity (11) ________ (to switch) (12) ________ to a new sport arose once winter came along the people of Montreal had no objection (13) ________ (to do) (14) ________ so.

*Lacrosse: A game invented by American Indians in which two teams try to propel a ball into each other's goal using long-handed rackets.

- **nach bestimmten Ausdrücken und nach bestimmten Verben**

  Beispiel: I can't stand working in the heat.

  Auch diese Liste solltest du gut lernen:

I dread seeing …	I denke mit Schrecken daran …
There is no point …	Es hat keinen Zweck/Sinn …
I can't bear …	Ich kann es nicht ertragen …
Do you fancy …	Haben Sie/Hast du Lust auf …
It is no good …	Es hat keinen Wert …
It's no use …	Es hat keinen Zweck …
to admit	zugeben
to appreciate	zu schätzen wissen
to avoid	vermeiden
to consider	erwägen
to delay	verschieben
to deny	leugnen, abstreiten
to dislike	etwas nicht mögen
to enjoy	genießen
to escape	flüchten, entfliehen
to excuse	entschuldigen
to finish	beenden
to forgive	verzeihen
to imagine	sich vorstellen
to involve	zur Folge haben, bedeuten
to mind	etwas haben gegen
to pardon	verzeihen
to postpone	verschieben
to regret	bedauern
to remember	sich erinnern
to resist	widerstehen
to risk	wagen, riskieren
to stop	aufhören
to suggest	vorschlagen
to understand	verstehen

Aufgabe 5 Build a full sentence with a gerund form in it. Use the phrases from the following list: *to take the money, to cross the road, to make such noise, to count your chickens before they're hatched, to cry over spilled milk, to listen to loud music.*

a)

It's no use ______________________

____

b) 

There's no point ____________
____

c) 

I can't stand ____________
____

d) 

I can't bear ____________
____

e) 

Do you admit ____________
____

f) 

Will you stop ____________
____________________________!

Aufgabe 6* **Mixed exercise:** Study the underlined gerund forms in the following passage and explain why each is used.

Heading slowly down the Information Highway

Learning about new technology is not as easy as it seems. Writing about the information superhighway recently, I was reminded of the many problems new technology can bring with it. The fact of the matter is that although the computer industry has generally succeeded in convincing people of the value of computers, the internet, cyperspace and so on, it is hard to change fundamental attitudes and behaviour. The latest developments in the realm of information technology have been radical to say the least. People however are not used to switching that fast. In other words just because something has been made technologically possible does not mean its effects will be seen overnight. On learning about new technology people need time to adapt to the changes this technology brings with it.

There is therefore little point in getting excited about the technology itself without first of all asking oneself how long it is likely to take for the world to become familiar with it. Doctors started switching over to computers only after coming out of medical schools that had started using computers. Up until the time medical schools went over to computers there was little progress made in bringing the medical profession round to the whole idea of using computers to help cure the ill. As well as mankind's inherent reluctance to change one must take into account the fact that things usually take longer to happen than one originally expects. It is hardly surprising that those who dream of one day achieving a world run by robots and computers now realize they may have to wait a little longer to see their dream come true.

Aufgabe 7 **Mixed exercise:** Read the following poem by Countee Cullen, then put together the questions you would ask the boy if the case went to court! Some take the gerund, others do not!

Incident by Countee Cullen

Once riding in old Baltimore,
Heart-filled, head-filled with glee,
I saw a Baltimorean;
Keep looking straight at me.

Now I was eight and very small,
And he was no whit bigger,
And so I smiled, but he poked out
His tongue, and called me, "Nigger."

I saw the whole of Baltimore
From May until December;
Of all the things that happened there
That's all that I remember.

no whit bigger = not one bit bigger, the same size as.
poked out = stuck out

Questions for the boy

a) you/remember/to see/Countee Cullen/Baltimore?
Do you remember seeing Countee Cullen in Baltimore on the day concerned?
I do.

b) you/deny/to call/her/a nigger?
____
I do.

c) you/usually/to play/black children?
____
I sometimes do.

d) you/to get/good grades/school?
____
Yes.

e) to be/you/habit of/to call/people/names?
____
____
No, I never do that.

f) you/enjoy/to hurt/people?
____
No, Sir. Not at all.

g) you / admit / to poke out / tongue / at her

____

____

I don't

h) to be / you / proud of / to be / white?

____

Yes, I am.

i) you / to mind / blacks / to get / good jobs?

____

____

Of course not.

j) you / to dislike / blacks / to have / money?

____

____

No, not in the slightest

k) your father / to employ / blacks?

____

____

Some.

l) you / to know / you are in danger / to go / jail / if found guilty?

____

____

Yes, I do.

Aufgabe 8 **A short test:** The following are examples of the kind of question your teacher might give you in a school test. See how many you get right!

Fill the gaps by putting in the verbs in the correct form. Sometimes a preposition is also needed.

a) By ___feeding___ (to feed) the bear she provided us with an opportunity ______________ (to see) the animal up close.

b) She left the building without ______________ (to say) goodbye.

c) ______________ (to play) in the woods is much nicer than ______________ (to work) indoors.

d) At first Tom liked ____________ (to talk) to her, but after a while he grew tired ____________ (to hear) the same dull stories over and over again. Now he would not want ____________ (to be) in any way similiar to her.

e) There's little point in ____________ (to buy) an expensive motorbike if you can't ____________ (to run) it.

Translation: Gerund or Infinitiv

f) Máiréad schlug vor, Eier zum Mittagessen zu kochen.

____

g) Die arme alte Frau sang weiter, obwohl keiner zuhörte.

____

h) Breda hasst es, spät ins Bett zu gehen.

____

i) Bitte vermeiden Sie es, Zigaretten auf den Boden zu werfen.

____

j) Harold riet ihr, das nie wieder zu sagen.

____

Aufgabe 9 **Gerund or infinitive:** In the following story you have to use the gerund or infinitive forms as you think correct. Sometimes a preposition is also necessary.

When Billy was young he dreamt (1) ____________ (to meet/meeting) the well-known footballer, Terry Goalscorer. He used wait outside the stadium after the match on a Saturday in the hope (2) ____________ (to see/seeing) Terry. Billy's mother warned him not (3) ____________ (to do/doing) that but he never obeyed her. She often heard him (4) ____________ (to sneak/sneaking) into the house at eight or nine o'clock on a Saturday evening. His father often allowed him (5) ____________ (to stay/staying) up late (6) ____________ (to watch/watching) recorded highlights of football games on TV. His mother however would come down the stairs in her nightgown and shout "I'm not keen (7) ____________ (to have/having) that lad in bad form tomorrow due to tiredness. Go to bed at once!"

After a League match one Saturday, as he stood outside Old Trafford Billy refused (8) ______________ (to go/going) home when his father called him. "I'm interested (9) ______________ (to talk/talking) to Terry Goalscorer" he shouted. "See you later". One hour later who should come out of the stadium but Terry Goalscorer. He signed an autograph for Billy, told him how he'd scored the winning goal with three minutes left (10) ______________ (playing/ to play) and how he hoped he'd see Billy again some time. When Billy told his parents his exciting news that evening they refused (11) ______________ (to believe/believing) a single word he said. "Imagine (12) ______________ (to say/saying) he met Terry Goalscorer! I suggest (13) ______________ (to take/taking) that boy to the doctor!", his mother complained that evening! Poor Billy! Life is tough with parents who won't believe you!

Aufgabe 10* Creative Writing

Compose a diary entry: You won a holiday for two people to Dublin, Ireland. It is late at night after a day around the city. Write a journal entry describing your day, the holiday so far and what you think of the country. Use the photos for ideas. In the course of your account try and include as many gerunds as possible.

9 Partizip Präsens und Partizip Perfekt

Im Englischen gibt es zwei Grundformen des Partizips: das **Partizip Präsens** *(present participle)* und das **Partizip Perfekt** *(past participle)*. Diese beiden Partizipien unterscheiden sich nicht zeitlich voneinander, sondern vielmehr darin, dass das Partizip Präsens **aktivische Bedeutung** und das Partizip Perfekt **passivische Bedeutung** hat.

Wann verwendest du die beiden Partizipien?

Für die beiden Partizipien gibt es eine ganze Reihe von Verwendungsmöglichkeiten:

- als **Adjektiv**
  Beispiele: The sleeping child.
  The stolen jewels.
- **in manchen Zeiten**, z. B. nach Zeiten in der Verlaufsform und nach dem Perfekt
  Beispiele: The plane is taking off.
  He had spoken well.
- als **Passivform** eines Verbes
  Beispiel: The money was brought to the bank.
- nach **Verben der Wahrnehmung**
  Beispiel: I heard John screaming.
- in folgenden **Konstruktionen:**
  catch/find + object + present participle
  Beispiel: I caught Tom smoking in the garden.
  be busy + present participle
  Beispiel: She is busy preparing her speech.
  have + object + participle
  Beispiel: I had him questioned last month.

Hauptsächlich aber werden die Partizipien dazu benutzt, **Sätze zu verkürzen**:

- zur **Vermeidung eines Nebensatzes**
  Beispiel: When he realized that the child was in danger he shouted.
  Realizing that the child was in danger he shouted.
- zur **Vermeidung eines Relativsatzes**
  Beispiel: Many farms which are run by old people fall into disuse.
  Many farms run by old people fall into disuse.
- anstelle einer **adverbialen Bestimmung**
  Beispiel: After we had played football, we went home.
  Having played football, we went home.

Wie bildest du die Partizipien?

- **Partizip Präsens:** Infinitiv + *-ing*
  Beispiel: While the boy was sleeping, his father read a book.
- **Partizip Perfekt:** Infinitiv + *-ed, -d* bzw. 3. Form der unregelmäßigen Verben
  Beispiel: *The room was cleaned with a hoover.*

Aufgabe 1 The author, for many years a drug addict, is describing what happened one day when, after taking an overdose, she decided to have a bath. In this exercise your task is to explain the use of the participles underlined in the text.

"By the time Pamela returned, steaming[1] water was cascading[2] down the hall stairs. She ran up to the landing only to find water gushing[3] even more furiously down the flight above. It was pouring[4] off the landing like a small waterfall. Finally, reaching[5] the upper bathroom she found me nodded out in the bath with one arm draped[6] over the side. She tried to pull the plug out but the water was too hot and she couldn't keep her arm in the water long enough. It was scalding[7] hot and, like a lobster, I was gradually being cooked[8]. I was quite oblivious of my state. Pamela thought that if she could pull me out of the tub the water level would go down and she could then get at the plug. She grabbed hold of my arm and began to pull, but my arm was so soapy it slipped right through her hands and she fell backwards, hitting[9] her head on the bidet and knocking herself out. Another twenty minutes elapsed before Pamela came to, another twenty minutes while the water poured like a cataract through the house. It was now running[10] out of the front door, through the garden and on to the street. By the time Pamela came round and got the plug out, the ceiling on the landing had collapsed[11] and the carpets were ruined[12], the walls of the children's rooms were caving in and Pamela's face was black and blue, covered with ugly, raw lumps."

(Faithfull by Marianne Faithfull p. 302)

1 ______________________________

2 ______________________________

3 ______________________________

4 ______________________________

5 ______________________________

6 ______________________________

7 ______________________________

8 ______________________________

9 ______________________________

10 ______________________________

11 ______________________________

12 ______________________________

Aufgabe 2 **Kimberley, South Africa:** Complete the sentences with the correct form of the verb in brackets.

Kimberley is a South African town (1) ______________ (to found) by men who came in search of fortune when diamonds were (2) ______________ (to discover) there. A lot of memorials are to be seen there, nearly all of them (3) ______________ (to build) over the past century. The number of people (4) ______________ (to live) there is close to 170,000 and the streets are full of people (5) ______________ (to chat) in a number of languages. Most of the wealth in South Africa lies in the hands of the descendants of the first whites (6) ______________ (to bring) to SA by the East Dutch Company. Over the years the blacks, (7) ______________ (to know) as a hard-working people, served the whites. The men and women (8) ______________ (to lead) the country away from that old apartheid system that existed until the end of the twentieth century have a very important job. Many people (9) ______________ (to live) in Kimberley are glad of the change and are (10) ______________ (to get) on with their lives.

Aufgabe 3 **Walt Whitman:** The participle as an adjective

Complete the sentences about the poet Walt Whitman by inserting the correct adjective:
annoyed/annoying; interested/interesting; loved/loving; worried/worrying; inspired/inspiring; confused/confusing; surprised/surprising;

a) Walt Whitman is one of America's most ______________ poets.

b) Born in 1819, he was a ______________ son who became a printer, a newspaper reporter and teacher.

c) His first novel had a ______________________ theme, the advocation of temperance i. e. not drinking alcohol.

d) His first collection of poetry, *Leaves of Grass,* showed how interested Whitman was in city life and in the language of the people who lived there. Occasionally, when ________________ if he would ever write great work, Whitman turned to prayer.

e) The critics did not like the book. They found it dull and many of them, __________________ by it, said they did not understand it.

f) ______________________ by what the critics wrote, Whitman nevertheless continued writing.

g) His most famous and ______________ poems are *O Captain! My Captain!* and *When Lilacs last in the Dooryard bloom'd.* Both were written about the death of President Lincoln.

Aufgabe 4 Rewrite the following sentences using a participle construction. They all refer to the photograph of Willie Mays in action. Sometimes two answers are possible.

a) As a child I saw Willie Mays who played for the New York Giants.

____

b) As he waited for the pitcher to throw the ball, he gripped his bat tightly.

____

c) As he crouched in anticipation, Yogi Berra, catcher of the New York Yankees, seemed sure all would go well.

____

d) After he had struck the baseball, Mays began to run.

____

e) To hit 660 home runs is not easy; but Willie Mays did so and thus became one of the most famous baseball players ever.

____

f) The baseball bat which he used can be seen today in a museum.

____

Aufgabe 5 **Rudyard Kipling:** Participles are often used to shorten sentences. Provide a participle construction instead of the relative or adverbial clauses.

On a US tour which was undertaken (1) (________________) in the year 1889, the writer Rudyard Kipling met Wolcott Balestier, a writer who was born (2) (________________) in the town of Battleboro and with whom Kipling later wrote the novel, *The Naulakha.* Balestier had a sister Caroline, who was known (3) (________________) for her beauty. Kipling fell in love and married her. When Kipling saw (4) (________________) his wife's native Vermont, he immediately wanted to live there. After they had built (5) (________________) a home in Battleboro, they settled down to what they hoped would be a happy life there. Because he wanted (6) (________________) peace and privacy to write his books, Kipling became a recluse.

After Kipling had written (7) (________________) *Jungle Book* and *Captains Courageous,* he got involved in a court case that shattered his life. Because he thought (8) (________________) he could no longer live in Vermont, he returned with his wife and daughters to England. After the family had lived (9) (__________) in England for a while they all decided to return to Vermont. It was a bad decision. Kipling's daughter Josephine caught pneumonia in the course of the trip and died. Because he realized (10) (______________) he could never go back there, Kipling decided to sell their home in Vermont. The family left Vermont forever and Kipling, a writer who was very interested (11) (______________) in children, never recovered from the loss.

Die Partizipien werden auch oft verwendet, um aus zwei Sätzen einen zu machen.
Beispiel: I heard the door bang. I turned around.
Hearing the door bang, I turned around.

Aufgabe 6 **Link the sentences:** In this exercise you must join the two sentences by using a participle construction. Can you identify the well-known singer involved?

a) His father supported a wife and six children. He often worked late into the night to earn more money.

____

b) As a child this singer dreamt of being a cowboy. He practised all the usual cowboy tricks and hoped, one day, to buy a ranch and loads of livestock.

____

c) During his time at Oaklahoma State agricultural college he worked hard. He studied late into the night to pass his exams.

____

d) He also loved singing. He played the guitar and composed country and western songs in his spare time.

____

e) As a musician he was very good. He soon came to the notice of a record company.

____

f) He became very famous. He sold more records than any other American solo artist.

____

g) He has written great songs like *The Dance, You May Be Right, We Shall Be Free*. He always tries to speak to and for ordinary folk.

____

h) Thanks to his wealth he also became a cowboy. He bought his family a 400 acre ranch in Nashville.

____

His name is ____________________.

Aufgabe 7* **Translation:** The following quotations are all based on an RDP report on the first year of the Mandela government in South Africa. Your task is to translate each sentence into English. The underlined words need a participle construction.

a) Diese kurze Broschure stellt einige der bisher ausgeführten Pilotprogramme dar. (*ausführen* = to carry out)

____

b) Die Finanzierung des RDP ist der wichtigste Baustein von allen. (*finanzieren* = to finance, to fund)

____

____

c) Südafrika braucht eine Kultur des Lernens.

____

____

d) Der Aufbau einer Kultur der Partnerschaft fängt gerade erst an.

____

____

Aufgabe 8 **Final check:** Replace the participle constructions in these sentences with another construction.

The North American Indian Travelling College's museum is situated on Cornwall Island. Entering (1) (__________________) the Log Cabin that houses the museum, the first item to catch the visitor's attention is the mannequin display. Signs showing (2) (__________________) what each mannequin represents explain certain aspects of a clanmother's family e. g. her chief, subchief and faithkeeper. The 'misconceptions' display details the mistaken beliefs continuing (3) (__________________) right down to the present day about the First Nation Indians.
After seeing (4) (After one has seen__________) the misconceptions display the visitor is greeted by the various headgear and belts of the Iroquois. Many Indians, realizing (5) (__________________) the need to record treaties, historic events and spiritual ceremonies, did so by means of a wampum belt made (6) (__________________) from quahog shell.
The next display contains artifacts of the Ojibwe and Cree Indians. The beadwork, leather and bark artifacts displayed (7) (__________________) in the museum clearly show that the Ojibwe and Cree belong to the Eastern Woodland Indians. The Eastern Indians have always used flowers, trees and plants as patterns for their decorations. Comparing (8) (__________________) them to many other tribes one sees they did not waste any part of the animal killed (9) (__________________), or the wood felled (10) (__________________), believing (11) (__________________) there was a purpose for everything.
The final display consists of Mohawk baskets. On leaving (12) (__________________) the museum the visitor should not forget to visit the Indian village nearby.

North American Indian Travelling College
R.R. # 3
Cornwall Island, Ontario
K6H 5R7
or
P.O. Box 273
Hogansburg, New York
13655
Phone: (613) 932-9452
Fax: 613-932-0092

TOURS

	with guide	without guide
Adult	$ 5.00	$ 2.50
Sr. or Student	$ 3.00	$ 1.50
Children	$ 1.00	$ .50

GROUP TOURS

15 - 100	$ 1.00 each
100 +	$ .50 each

… rund um den Satz

10 *if*-Sätze

Ein **Bedingungssatz** *(conditional sentence)* ist ein Nebensatz, der die Voraussetzung oder Bedingung nennt, unter der das im Hauptsatz genannte Geschehen wahr wird.

Wann verwendest du *if*-Sätze?

Du verwendest ***if-clauses***, wenn du **Bedingungen** ausdrücken willst.

Beispiel: If I meet the postman, I will give him his Christmas present.
Bedingung — mögliche Folge

Wie bildest du *if*-Sätze?

Mit dem ***if*-Satz** (Nebensatz = *subordinate clause*) drückst du die **Bedingung** und mit dem **Hauptsatz** *(main clause)* die **mögliche Folge** aus.

Beispiel: If I go to school, I will meet Sally.
Bedingung / *if*-Satz — mögliche Folge / Hauptsatz

- **Erfüllbare (reale) Bedingungssätze**
  Im ***if*-Satz** steht eine **Bedingung, die erfüllt werden kann**.
  Beispiel: If you win the competition, we will go on a holiday.
  if-Satz: *present tense* — Hauptsatz: *will-future*
- **Unwahrscheinliche Bedingungssätze**
  Im ***if*-Satz** steht eine **Bedingung**, deren **Erfüllung** man eher für **unwahrscheinlich** hält.
  Beispiel: If you won the competition, we would go on a holiday.
  if-Satz: *past tense* — Hauptsatz: *conditional*
- **Irreale Bedingungssätze**
  Im ***if*-Satz** steht eine **Bedingung, die nicht mehr erfüllt werden kann**, da sie sich auf die Vergangenheit bezieht. Somit stellt diese „Bedingung" eine bloße Annahme dar.
  Beispiel: If you had won the competition, we would have gone on …
  if-Satz: *past perfect* — Hauptsatz: *conditional perfect*

Aufgabe 1 **Vocabulary:** Check the meaning of the following words in your dictionary.

a) to encourage ______

b) a splint ______

c) to refer someone ______

d) a wallet ______

e) ransom demand ______

f) debt ______

g) wireless ______

Aufgabe 2

Now suggest the correct action the doctor should take in these situations. Give 3 answers like in the example.

Beispiel:
If the patient feels hot I will take her temperature.
If the patient felt hot I would take her temperature.
If the patient had felt hot I would have taken her temperature.

a) to have a pain in her tummy — to ask about her diet

______

______

______

b) to feel very dizzy — to tell her to sit down

______

______

______

c) to twist his ankle — to send him for an x-ray

______

______

______

d) to suffer a broken leg — to make a splint for him

______

______

______

e) to need an immediate operation — to call an ambulance

______

______

______

f) to smoke too much — to encourage him to stop

______

______

______

Aufgabe 3 Explain what the following would do if these situations occurred.

a)

If a thief saw a wallet he ______

______

______

b)

If Marie got lost ______

______

______

c)

If the postman saw a fierce ____________________

____

d)

If the baby cried its father ____________________

____

Aufgabe 4 Now in this exercise you must say what would (not) have happened if the person had not done what they did.

a)

If the thief had not stolen the wallet ________

____

____

b)

If Marie had not asked the way ________________

____

c) 

If the postman had not
________________the dog
____

d) 

If the father had not
____
____

Aufgabe 5 **Jan van Riebeeck's Hedge:** Read the following text and then answer the questions.

The first white settlers to set foot in South Africa landed at the Cape of Good Hope in 1652. They were working for the Dutch East India Company which was interested in the Cape as a place where ships could take food and water on board on their way to the rich lands of the East. Jan van Riebeeck, the settlers' leader, was under orders to buy cattle from local farmers but otherwise to have nothing to do with the natives.

These natives, who were known as the Khoikhoi people, were hunters and cattle farmers. They became angry when the Dutch began taking more and more land from them. In his diary van Riebeeck wrote "they asked if they would be allowed to do such a thing if they went to Holland".

In 1660 Van Riebeeck planted a hedge on the side of Table Mountain as a fence between the settlers and the Khoikhoi. The hedge was the perfect way of cutting off the two communities from one another. Inside this hedge a small European community grew up 6,000 miles from home. Van Riebeeck could not get the natives to work for the Dutch so some of the settlers were given land to produce food the Company might buy. These farmers became known as "boers" – a name still used to describe their grandchildren in South Africa today.

a) **Language:** Write down the words in the text for:
- something built to close off gardens and fields ______________________
- people who come to live in a place ______________________
- a daily record of personal events ______________________

Use the words in brackets to make nouns and write them down.
- The film director had to raise extra money to finish the ____________ (to produce).
- The jury was unable to find the man guilty due to lack of ____________ (to prove).

b) **if-clauses:** Fill in the correct forms.
- If I see him I ______________________ (to tell) him the news.
- If you ______________ (to listen) to me you would learn something.
- If you ______________________ (not stop) smoking you're days are numbered.
- If I ______________________ (to hear) the telephone ringing I would have answered it.
- If you ________________ (to play) with the boy he will be happier.
- If she had really loved him she ______________________ (to let) him go to Crewe.

c) **Translation:** Translate the following into German.
If Van Riebeeck knew the land belonged to the natives why did he take it from them?
If Van Riebeeck had felt truly sorry for them he would have done far more for them.
If he had spoken nicely to them and had never taken their land they would not have asked him whether they would be allowed to do the same in Holland.

Aufgabe 6* **Figures of speech:** What will happen to Anne if she does/doesn't do her homework? Look at the pictures and write down the appropriate figure of speech so that it fits in the sentences and matches the picture. Then pick the definition from the list that explains the figure of speech.

Figures of speech: *to get into hot water, to give someone the cold shoulder, to face the music, to be the apple of someone's eye, to be under a cloud, to turn over a new leaf, to swing the lead.*

Definitions: *to ignore or not talk to someone, to get into trouble, to start afresh, to be a person's pride and joy, to confront the results of one's actions, to be in a state of gloom suspicion or scandal, to be lazy and do no work.*

a)

If she doesn't do her homework she will have to face the music.

Definition: To confront the results of one's actions.

b)

If she doesn't do her homework ______________________

Definition: ______________________

c)

If she doesn't do her homework her father ______________________

Definition: ______________________

d)

If she doesn't do her homework she ______________________

Definition: ______________________

Normalerweise darfst du *would* und *should* im *if*-Satz nicht verwenden. Es gibt aber zwei Ausnahmen:

- besonders **höfliche Aufforderung oder Bitte**

  Beispiel: If you would be so kind to loan me some cash I'd be very grateful.
  if-Satz: *should* oder *would* Hauptsatz: *future* oder *conditional*

- etwas erscheint **besonders unwahrscheinlich**

  Beispiel: If you should have any questions do not hesitate to call me.
  if-Satz: *should* oder *would* Hauptsatz: *future* oder *conditional*

Aufgabe 7 Insert the words *should* or *would* as you see fit.

a) If you ____________________ have any trouble getting replacement fittings let me know.

b) If you ____________________ wait a moment I'll inform my boss you're here.

c) I would be very grateful if you ____________________ arrange a meeting.

d) If you ____________________ happen to see him tell him to ring me.

e) If you ____________________ just sign on the dotted line the deal will be complete.

f) If you ____________________ kindly open your folders we will begin.

g) If these goods ____________________ not be to your satisfaction in any way we will gladly replace them.

h) ____________________ this suggestion not be suitable please let us know.

i) If Peter ____________________ make up his mind which film he wants to see we could get going.

j) If you ____________________ care to meet her I'll introduce you.

k) If you ____________________ be interested in the job ring Mr Scholes.

Aufgabe 8 Many people would have done things differently had they had certain information at vital times in their lives. Complete the following by building answers using the words given.

a) 

(not go to Dallas)
If he had known his enemies were plotting to kill him he ______________________.

b) 

(not marry her)
If he had known his marriage to Diana would be an unhappy one he ______________________.

c) 

(not leave the hotel)
If he had known an armed man was waiting for him he ______________________.

d) 

(sow other crops)
If the people of Ireland had known the potato crop was going to fail in 1845 they ______________________
______________________.

Aufgabe 9 Complete the sentences to uncover the period.

a) If you had lived at that time you (not, to know) ______________________ how to drive a car.

b) If you had lived in those days you (not, to hear) ______________________ of television.

c) If you had lived in this country at that time then you (to speak) ______________________ what we would now call old-fashioned English.

d) If you had lived in the south of the country you (to be) ______________________ either very rich or very poor.

e) If you had lived in the north of the country you (to disagree) ____________ with one important aspect of southern life.

f) If you had lived at that time then you (to have to decide) ________________ whether to support the men in blue or the men in grey.

g) If you had lived in the north of this country you (to be prepared) ______________________ to die for man's freedom.

h) If you had lived in that century you (to see) ____________________ many battles.

Name the period and the place! ____________________________

Aufgabe 10 **Mixed test:** Fill in the correct forms.

a) If you want to see the Rolling Stones live this year, you (to have) ____________________ to go to London.

b) If we write for tickets now we (to find out) ______________________ what they cost.

c) If you ____________________ (to work) too hard you will not enjoy the concert.

d) If you speak only German while in England you ______________________ (to learn) very little English.

e) If you should pass your driving test I ______________________ (to throw) a party in your honour.

f) If they had placed the order earlier they ______________________ (to have) the goods now.

g) If the snow (not to fall) ____________________ we could have avoided the accident.

h) If Tom had spoken sooner I (to give) ____________________ him the job.

i) We ______________ (go) to the beach, if the weather __________________ (be) nice tomorrow.

j) If Marconi had not invented the wireless, he __________________________ (not, to become) famous.

k) The criminals would have killed the boy, if his father __________________ (not, pay) the ransom demand.

l) If I __________________ (be) a French, I __________________ (can, speak) perfect French.

11 Relativpronomen und Relativsätze

Relativpronomen (*who, that, whose, which* etc.) sind Pronomen, die einen Nebensatz, genauer gesagt einen **Relativsatz**, einleiten und ihn auf ein oder mehrere Nomen oder Pronomen des Hauptsatzes beziehen.

11.1 Relativpronomen

Wann verwendest du welches Relativpronomen?

- ***who*** wird nur für **Personen** verwandt und kann im Relativsatz sowohl **Subjekt** als auch **Objekt** sein.

  Beispiel: This is the man who broke his leg.

- ***which*** wird du nur für **Dinge** gebraucht und kann ebenfalls **Subjekt** oder **Objekt** eines Relativsatzes sein.

  Beispiel: Is this the record which cost 10 pounds?

- ***that*** wird für **Personen** und **Dinge** benutzt. Auch hier ist ein Einsatz als **Subjekt** oder **Objekt** im Relativsatz möglich.

  Beispiele: The policeman that found it was very nice.
  The money that I lost was in my pocket.

- ***whom*** bezieht sich ausschließlich auf **Personen** und kann nur **Objekt** eines Relativsatzes sein. Im Schrift-Englisch wird *whom* oft zusammen mit einer Präposition benutzt.

  Beispiele: Mary, whom I have known all my life, is a good friend.
  The man to whom she was speaking is French.

- ***where*** leitet Relativsätze ein, die eine **Richtung** oder einen **Ort** beschreiben. Es kann sowohl als **Subjekt** als auch als **Objekt** des Relativsatzes eingesetzt werden.

  Beispiele: The pool where we used to go swimming has been closed.
  This is the house where Wordsworth was born.

- ***whose*** kennzeichnet eine **Zugehörigkeit** oder einen **Besitz** und kann sowohl für **Personen** als auch für **Dinge** gebraucht werden. Außerdem kann *whose* **Subjekt** oder **Objekt** des Relativsatzes sein. Verwechselt werden darf *whose* aber nicht mit *who's*, der Kurzform von *who is*.

  Beispiele: The builder, whose company built my house, is a rich man.
  The cars whose tyres were slashed were parked at the hotel.

Aufgabe 1 *who, which, whom, that, whose, where*: Study the photograph and then make one sentence of the two.

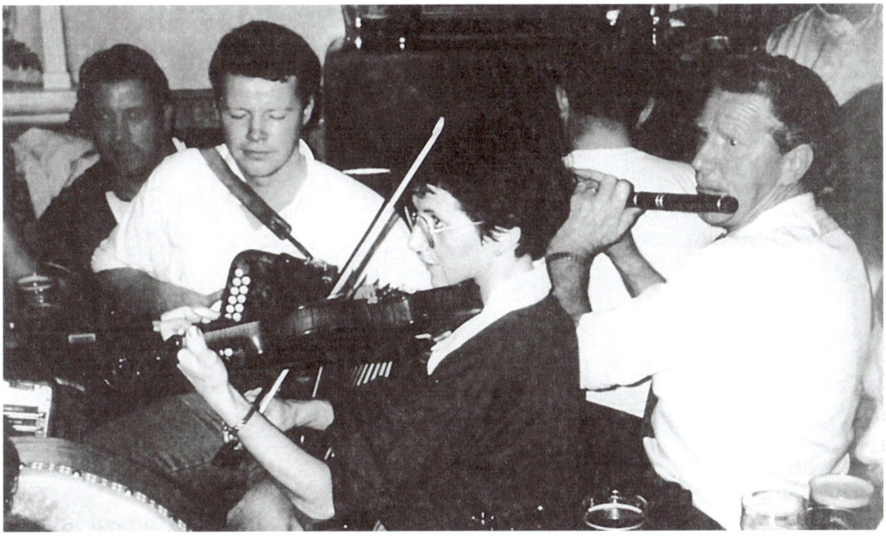

a) Clonmel is the name of a town in Ireland. This music session took place there.

Clonmel is the name of the town in Ireland where this music session took place.

b) The woman is playing the fiddle. She bought it years ago.

c) Who is that man? His eyes are closed.

d) The bow is a long stick. The fiddler is holding it in her right hand.

e) These musicians were attending the Fleadh Cheoil, an important Irish music festival. The photographer saw them in a pub.

f) The publican asked these musicians to play. He was very pleased he did so.

____

____

g) The two men are playing with the fiddler. They know her well.

____

____

h) Folk music is popular throughout Ireland. It is played in pubs, on street corners and at festivals.

____

____

Aufgabe 2 The professions: *who* or *who's* or *whose?* Fill in the correct form.

a) A blacksmith is a person _______________ job it is to shoe horses.

b) An actor is a man _______________ has to memorize thousands of lines.

c) Anyone _______________ feet are sore should go to a chiropodist.

d) _______________ that woman over there? That's the local headmistress.

e) Which one do you mean? The one _______________ standing by the door or the woman _______________ shirt is torn.

f) Can you do anything for a child _______________ father has forgotten her medical card?

g) A plumber is a man or woman _______________ knows all about heating and water systems.

h) That's the nurse _______________ daughter recently married a doctor.

Aufgabe 3 Connect the following sentences using a relative pronoun.

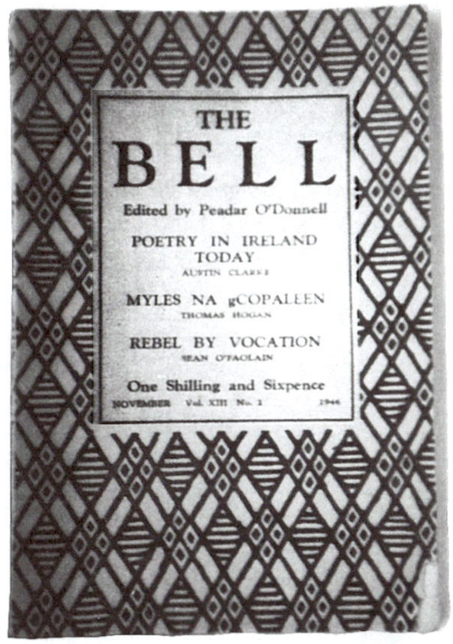

a) Ireland is a small country. Poetry is very important there.

b) Ireland has many literary magazines. They publish both Irish and non-Irish writers.

c) Sean O'Faoláin was a famous Irish writer. He published *The Bell* in the 1940s and 1950s.

d) *Innti* is a well-known publication. It publishes poetry written in the Irish language.

e) *The Honest Ulsterman* is published in Belfast. Many famous Irish poets started writing in Belfast.

f) *Metre* is a Dublin magazine. It often publishes translations of European poetry.

g) The editor of *Krino* is Gerald Dawe. He is also a poet.

h) *Poetry Ireland Review* is probably Ireland's best known poetry magazine. Many writers and poets submit to it.

11.2 Relativsätze

Welche Arten von Relativsätzen gibt es?

- **notwendiger Relativsatz**
  Ein notwendiger Relativsatz *(defining relative clause)* **bestimmt** das Wort **genauer**, auf das er sich bezieht. Ohne die Informationen, die der notwendige Relativsatz liefert, ist der Hauptsatz nicht verständlich. Der notwendige Relativsatz steht ohne Kommas.

  Beispiel: That is the policeman who stopped me last night.
  (In diesem Beispiel handelt es sich nicht um irgendeinen Polizisten, sondern um genau den, der mich letzte Nacht angehalten hat. Hieße der Satz *That is the policeman* würde jeder wissen wollen, was mit dem Polizisten los ist.)

- **nicht notwendiger Relativsatz**
  Ein nicht notwendiger Relativsatz *(non-defining relative clause)* gibt **zusätzliche Informationen** zu dem Wort, auf das er sich bezieht. Auch ohne diese Zusatzinformationen wäre der Satz verständlich. Der nicht notwendige Relativsatz wird vom Rest des Satzes durch Kommas abgetrennt.

  Beispiel: My sister, whose husband is French, lives in Cornwall.
  (Würde der Satz *My sister lives in Cornwall* lauten, wäre die Aussage des Satzes ebenso klar. Dass der Ehemann meiner Schwester Franzose ist, stellt nur eine zusätzliche Information dar.)

Welche Relativpronomen verwendest du in welchen Arten von Relativsätzen?

	notwendiger R.-Satz		nicht notwendiger R.-Satz	
	Personen	Dinge	Personen	Dinge
Subjekt	who /that	which /that	who	which
Objekt	whom /who /that	which /that	who(m)	which
Possessiv	whose	whose /of which	whose	whose /of which

Aufgabe 4 **A mixed bag of relative clauses:** In each sentence in Box 1 a relative clause has been left out. Your task is to choose a relative clause from the Box 2 that matches the sentence in Box 1. Then put the missing word into each clause.

Box 1

A Quebec, *which is mainly French-speaking*, is also the largest province in Canada.

B Michael Jackson, ______________________, is a rich man.

C Sarah Ferguson, ______________________, is the former wife of Prince Andrew.

D My glasses, ______________________, don't suit me that well.

E Tom's girlfriend, ______________________________, has a great job.

F The latest inflation figures, ______________________________, are worrying.

G This painting, ______________________________, is very dear.

H The song *My Way*, ______________________________, will always belong to Frank Sinatra.

Box 2

1 the frame ____________ ____________ is missing

2 ____________ were issued by the government today

3 ____________ ____________ there are hundreds of versions

4 ____________ mother is ill

5 ____________ I bought last month

6 ____________ comes from a musical family

7 ____________ is also a cartoonist

8 ____________ is mainly French-speaking

Aufgabe 5 **Female American fiction:** In the following exercise you have to simply decide whether the relative clause is a defining or non-defining one. You should also put in the commas when needed.

a) 

Willa Cather who wrote *O Pioneers* and eleven other books not to mention 58 stories is generally acknowledged as one of the major American fiction writers of this century.

____

____

b) Louise Edrich is a writer who has a very large readership and has been translated into many languages.

____

c) American works of fiction such as *In Country* which launched Bobbie Ann Mason's career are giving female fiction in America a good name.

____

____

____

____

d) Alice Walker and Alison Lurie both of whom won the Pulitzer Prize for fiction in the 1980s are two names that come to mind when discussing important fiction in recent years.

____

e) The short story is an important literary form which is enjoying a revival at present.

____

f) 

Ann Castillo is a Hispanic writer who started publishing with small Hispanic presses in the US before moving to larger publishing houses.

____

____

g) Female writers who write mainly to fight for women's rights have been loudly criticized by many male critics and writers.

____

h) The imput of female American writers today many of whom have won important prizes for their work has been commented on by various observers.

____

- Ist das **Relativpronomen direktes Objekt** eines Relativsatzes, kann es auch **weggelassen** werden.

  Beispiel: The car that he bought was cheap.
  The car he bought was cheap.

- Wenn das Relativpronomen *that* gebraucht wird, muss die Präposition nach das Verb gestellt werden. Bei den anderen Relativpronomen kann die Präposition sowohl vor dem Relativpronomen als auch nach dem Verb stehen.

  Beispiele: The bus that he arrived on was late.
  The bus on which he arrived was late.
  The bus which he arrived on was late.

Aufgabe 6 Each of the six statements below might be used in written English. Your task is to complete them and then find two easier ways of saying the same thing.

a) The woman _at_ _whom_ O'Brien is looking is called Deirdre.
The woman O'Brien ____________________

____

b) The park bench ________ ________ they are sitting was bought by the corporation.

____

____

c) The man ________ ________ the girl is engaged works in the E.S.B.

____

____

d) The magazine ________ ________ she is leafing is a woman's magazine.

____

____

e) The things ________ ________ he is thinking change suddenly.

____

____

f) The pub ________ ___________ O'Brien is going is called O'Reilly's.

____

____

Aufgabe 7 **The End of the World:** Fill in the correct relative pronouns, if necessary.

Over the centuries there have been many people (1) ___________ have forecast the end of the world. Many (2) ___________ predictions were believed by their contemporaries have been proven wrong by time itself. Take the Book of Revelations for instance. Early Christians assumed the apocalypse would occur in their own lifetime. That's one prediction (3) ___________ has not come true! In the 1840s, William Miller, a man (4) _________ had thousands of followers, turned to calculation and the Bible for the date everyone wanted to know. The Bible, a book (5) ___________ he was well-acquainted with, contained the answer. Or so he claimed. Taking words and numbers from the book he calculated that 1843 was the year in question. Miller, (6) ___________ reputation was at its highpoint when he said this, was also shown to be incorrect. James Usher, an Irish archbishop is another (7) ___________ time has proven wrong. His prediction, (8) ___________ was October, 1996, has also met its match.
North Yorkshire was the place (9) ___________ Mother Shipton was born. She predicted many things (10) ___________ have since come true. Aeroplanes for example. But the end of the world was too much for even a woman like Mother Shipton, (11) ___________________ is remembered to this day by Yorkshire folk. The world "to an end shall come", she announced, "in eighteen hundred and eighty one."
Which leaves us with a number of candidates (12) ___________ predictions may yet come true and (13) _____________ may earn short-lived fame. Nostradamus, about (14) ___________ we know very little, forecast that in July 1999 the end of the world would take place. David Icke tipped 1997, Andrew Jackson, (15) ___________ prediction was a little vague said "around 2000". They too were wrong. (16) ___________ knows when the end will come!
(17) __________ seems to prove that we just don't know when this dreadful event will happen is that every day a new forecast is made. Or maybe it won't happen at all. After all, as the saying goes, "All's well (18) __________ ends well."

Aufgabe 8 Compose eight sentences about the following cartoon which all include a relative clause. After you have thought of each sentence write it another way as is done in the example.

a) The man *who is speaking to the Prime Minister* works in Downing Street.

The man speaking to the Prime Minister works in Downing Street.

b) The box ______________________________

____

c) The woman ______________________________

____

d) The curtains ______________________________

____

e) The picture ______________________________

____

f) The children ______________________________

____

g) The table

h)

i)

Aufgabe 9*

Creative Writing

Study the photos here. Imagine you live in a fishing village in England or Ireland. Describe life in your village. What is it like to live there? How would life be different if you lived in a city? What do you do in the village if the weather is good, stormy etc? Use as many if clauses as possible.

12 Indirekte Rede

Die indirekte Rede *(reported speech)* ist ein Form der **Redeerwähnung:** Innerhalb einer Äußerung wird auf eine andere Äußerung eingegangen.

Wann verwendest du die indirekte Rede?

Du verwendest die indirekte Rede, wenn du das, was ein anderer gesagt hat, wiedergeben willst.

Beispiel: The president said, "The people can rely on me."
(direkt speech)
The President said (that) the people could rely on him.
(reported speech)

Wie bildest du die indirekte Rede?

Du bildest die **indirekte Rede** aus einem **Einleitungssatz mit Einleitungsverben** wie *say*, *ask*, *report* und einem ***that*-Satz**.

Beispiel: Tom: "Who hurt the cat?"
(direkt speech)
Tom wanted to know who had hurt the cat.
(reported speech)

Die einzelnen Regeln, die du bei der Bildung der indirekten Rede beachten musst, werden dir auf den folgenden Seiten erklärt. Zuvor solltest du aber diese Verben gründlich lernen. Sie werden häufig verwendet, um eine indirekte Rede einzuleiten: *to add, to admit, to agree, to announce, to ask, to declare, to emphasize, to explain, to notice, to order, to promise, to regret, to reply, to remark, to report, to say, to shout, to state, to suggest, to tell, to threaten, to want to know, to warn.*

Rund um die Verwendung der Zeiten, der Pronomen und Adverbien in der indirekten Rede

- **direkte Rede im Präsens oder im Futur**
  Steht das **Einleitungsverb** im ***present tense*** oder im ***future tense***, so bleiben die **Zeiten** der direkten Rede in der indirekten Rede **unverändert**.

  Beispiel: Helen: "The boy is at school" *(direkt speech)*
  Helen says the boy is at school *(reported speech)*

- **direkte Rede in der Vergangenheit**
  Steht das **Einleitungsverb** in der *past tense*, so werden die **Zeiten** der direkten Rede in der indirekten folgendermaßen **verschoben:**

  simple present → simple past
  Beispiel: The man: "I love horror movies".
  The man said he loved horror movies.

  present progressive → past progressiv
  Beispiel: The man: "They are showing a horror movie in the cinema."
  The man said they were showing a horror movie in the cinema.

  simple past → past perfect
  Beispiel: "I loved horror movies when I was young".
  The man said he had loved horror movies when he had been young.

  will-future → conditional
  Beispiel: The woman: "The boy will be frightened by it".
  The woman said the boy would be frightened by it.

  future continuous → conditional progressive
  Beispiel: "The Roxy will be showing horror movies next year."
  The manager declared that the Roxy would be showing horror movies the year after that.

  Ausnahme: Allgemeingültige Tatsachen können sowohl im *present tense* als auch im *past tense* wiedergegeben werden.
  Beispiel: "Reading broadens the mind."
  The librarian said reading broadens the mind.
  The librarian said that reading broadened the mind.

- **Pronomen und Adverbiale**
  Pronomen und Adverbiale müssen dem Standpunkt des neuen Erzählers angepasst werden.

  Personalpronomen
  I/you/we/you → he/she/they
  Beispiel: "I will go home."
  She/he said that he/she would go home.

  Possessivbegleiter
  my/your/our/your → his/her/their
  Beispiel: "My Dad arrived last week."
  He/She said his/her Dad had arrived the week before.

  Demonstrativpronomen
  this/these → that/those
  Beispiel: "This is my pen."
  He/She said that was his/her pen.

Orts- und Zeitangaben

today → *that day*
yesterday → *the day before*
last week → *the week before (the same with month, year, etc.)*
ago → *before (that)*
now → *then*
here → *there*

Beispiel: "It was wet yesterday."
He/She said it had been wet the day before.

Aufgabe 1 Leonard Bone drives vintage cars. He loves nothing better than to be behind the wheel of a Ford Morris, Rolls Royce or Bentley Fiat. Recently he took a friend, Enda Fynes, for a spin. These are some of the things they said to each other in the course of the trip. Put them into reported speech.

a) This Model T Ford is my favourite vintage car.
Leonard said ______________________________

b) I took it out for a short spin last week.
Leonard told Enda ______________________________

c) Our grandfather bought the car a long time ago.
Leonard ______________________________

d) We had better jump in now because it's time to go.
Leonard ______________________________

e) These old cars are fantastic.
Enda ______________________________

f) This is the lucky charm my grandfather always wore when driving.
Leonard ______________________________

g) I checked the brakes yesterday.
Leonard ______________________________

h) This is great fun!
Enda ______________________________

i) As kids we loved cleaning this car.
Leonard ______________________________

j) Your grandfather took good care of this car.
Enda ______________________________

k) I'll start now. Hold on to your hat!
Leonard ______________________________

l) We will be in Navan soon.
Enda ______________________________

Aufgabe 2 Sgt. Pepper! Listening to her favourite rock programme on BBC Radio 1, Helen Carter hears the D. J. talking about the album Sgt. Pepper's Lonely Hearts Club Band. He tells his audience some unusual things about the album. Next day Helen talks to her friend Lucy in school. Complete the sentences in line with the example.

THE BEATLES STORY

a) "'When I'm Sixty-Four' was a very early Paul McCartney composition."
The D. J. said that 'When I'm Sixty-Four' had been a very early Paul McCartney composition.

b) "The sound effects on Lovely Rita were created by using combs and toilet paper. Once The Beatles recorded the sounds they played them backwards and liked what they heard!"
He maintained ____________________

c) "Actress Mae West at first refused to allow her image to appear on the album cover. She went back on her initial decision after the Beatles wrote to her."
The guy claimed ____________________

d) "A Day in the Life was banned by the B.B.C."
I already knew ____________________

e) "Spiro Agnew, the well-known American politician, led a crusade to ban 'With a Little Help from My Friends'."
He explained ____________________

f) "A TV commercial for Kellogs' Cornflakes inspired John Lennon to write 'Good Morning, Good Morning'."
He related the funny tale of how ____________________

g) "John Lennon found the lyrics for 'Being for the Benefit of Mr Kite' on an antique poster which was used in 1843 to advertize a circus in Rochdale."
He explained ____________________

h) "It hasn't taken the album long to sell more than ten million copies worldwide and that must be a record!"
He finished by saying that ____________________

i) "The man who blew his mind out in a car in 'A Day in the Life' was Tars Browne, heir to the Guinness fortune."
He also mentioned ______________________________

____

- **Hilfsverben**
  Hilfsverben müssen ebenso verändert werden:

  may → might
  Beispiel: Kevin: "May I leave the room?"
  Kevin asked if he might leave the room.

  can → could
  Beispiel: Kelly: "Can you drive?"
  Kelly asked if I could drive.

  must → had to (Notwendigkeit)
  Beispiel: Tom: "I must go."
  Tom said he had to go.

  must → must (Annahme)
  Beispiel: Ann: "I must have been there by 6 p. m."
  Ann declared she must have been there by 6 p. m.

Aufgabe 3 **Seamus Heaney:** Seamus Heaney won the Nobel Prize for Literature in 1995. Complete the task by changing what people said at the time about his win into indirect speech.

a) "The guardian spirit of Irish poetry has like his predecessor, Yeats, received his just recognition."
Derek Walcott said that the guardian spirit of Irish poetry had like his predecessor, Yeats, received his just recognition.

b) "Today's announcement is especially exciting because Seamus is in the middle of his best work."
Publisher Peter Fallon said ______________________________

c) "I felt very emotional, tears came and it was a mixture of joy and sadness, for the old times."
His sister Anne said ______________________________

d) "The last time I saw him, four months ago, he charmed a 2,000 strong audience of A/Level students."
The poet Blake Morrison wrote ______________________________

e) "At first I thought I must be dreaming. Now I am thrilled to be here representing the Irish Government at this time."
Mr Toddy O'Sullivan in Stockholm said ______________________________

f) "Much will be made of the fact that the prize has gone to a Northern poet who has chosen to make his home in the South; and no doubt there will be mutterings from many quarters that the Nobel committee has once again made a political choice by awarding the prize to an Irishman at the end of a year which has been one of the most hopeful yet perilously balanced periods in the history of our two states."
The Irish Times stated that ______________________________

g) "I must buy his book *The Spirit Level* tomorrow."
A Dubliner questioned in O'Connell Street said ______________________________

Rund um Fragen in der indirekten Rede

- Sind in Fragen in der indirekten Rede **Fragewörter** wie *who, what, why, when, how* enthalten, so werden diese in der indirekten Rede **wiederholt**.

  Beispiel: "Who broke the window?"
  He wanted to know who had broken the window.

- In **Entscheidungsfragen**, in der ja in der direkten Rede keine Fragewörter enthalten sind, wird die **indirekte Rede mit *if* oder *whether* eingeleitet**.

  Beispiel: "Is Tim ill?"
  She asked if Tim was ill.

Aufgabe 4

George Washington:

In the following conversation George Washington is giving a brief account of his life.

„My great-grandfather emigrated from England in protest after King George I was defeated by Cromwell. My family has been living here in Virginia now for many years. We own a lot of land along the Potomac. Mathematics was my favourite subject at school. My father died when I was a teenager so I came to look on my brother Lawrence as my closest relative. Unfortunately, he too passed away some years ago. At the age of 19 I became a wealthy landowner. In 1753, I was commissioned to visit and deliver a letter to the French forces on the Ohio. That must have been my first test as a military leader. A long time ago all I wanted was to acquire land but that trip stirred a real sense of patriotism in me. And I'll tell you something else; I might never have become a general were it not for my wife! She gave me wonderful support all my life and I have loved her two children as if they were my own. I will be very surprised if the colonies don't become independent in the course of my lifetime. I only hope they will do so without bloodshed."

Turn the above paragraph into Reported Speech. Start like this:
George Washinton told the audience (that) ...

Aufgabe 5 In the course of his conversation George Washington was asked a number of questions by his audience. Among these were:

a) "Did you get on well with your father?"
b) "Has your family always lived in Virginia?"
c) "Is your mother still alive?"
d) "How did your brother Lawrence die?"
e) "How long have you known your wife?"
f) "What do you think of the British Stamp Act?"
g) "Is it hard to be a British subject living in Virginia?"
h) "Are you friends with General Forbes?"
i) "Do you intend to go back to farming?"
j) "Will the colonies ever become independent?"
k) "Would you be prepared to fight the British?"
l) "Will you dine with us tonight?"
m) "When will you see your family again?"

n) "Do you read much?"
o) "Who is your favourite writer?"

After George Washington had finished, he went home. There he told his wife what he had been asked. Turn the answers into indirect speech.

a) He asked me if I had got on well with my father?
b) She enquired if
c) One man asked
d)
e)
f)
g)
h)
i)
j)
k)
l)
m)
n)
o)

Rund um Aufforderungen, Bitten und Ratschläge in der indirekten Rede

In der indirekten Rede werden **Aufforderungen, Bitten** und **Ratschläge** durch eine **Infinitiv-Konstruktion** wiedergegeben.

Beispiele: "Do the work now!"
The manager instructed him to do the work then.
"Give me the money please."
The girl asked me to please give her the money.
"Don't eat too much!"
His Daddy advised him not to eat too much.

Aufgabe 6 **Robert E. Peary:** Robert E. Peary was one of the most famous explorers of all time. During the course of his expeditions to the North Pole he had cause to give advice and instructions to the teams that accompanied him. The following list consists of things Peary wrote or said. Statement n is a quote from a letter Peary got from his wife. Turn each sentence into Reported Speech. Use verbs like *to order, to instruct, to urge, to warn, to ask, to beg.*

a) "Push on with all possible speed."
Peary advised the others to push on with all possible speed.

b) "Don't let me sleep for longer than 4 hours."

c) "Overhaul and strengthen the sledges."

d) "Set your course by the moon."

e) "Do not camp here."

f) "Cross the lead."

g) "Overtake us and give us fuel."

h) "You must cover 30 miles tomorrow."

i) "Don't ever travel without women!"

j) "Turn in and sleep."

k) "Be sure and rest the dogs."

l) "Don't worry too much."

m) "Tell me when the sun is up."

____

n) "You must come home!"

____

Aufgabe 7 **Reported speech in school tests!** During your year in Class Nine there's a very good chance reported speech will form some part of a school test. The following exercise is one such example. Rewrite these statements in reported speech. Start each sentence with a different introductory verb in the past tense. Do not use *say*!

Extract from a TV Programme

a) PRESENTER: A series of bomb hoaxes threw the London underground into chaos this morning. Across the city people on their way to work were left stranded as police cleared eight railway stations in the capital. The loss to the economy in earnings and production will not be known until later this week but it is estimated to run into millions of pounds. Police are asking for help with the investigation and this afternoon a hotline number was set up. Can you help? A police constable is waiting 24 hours a day to take your call. You just might have seen or heard something that would lead to an arrest. The number to ring is 0171–565677.

b) FIRST LONDONER: Who does this sort of thing? Is it a crackpot or is this 9/11 all over again. Whoever it is they must be sick. I was on my way to work when it happened. I ended up four hours late.

c) SECOND LONDONER: I can't understand these people.

d) THIRD LONDONER: Is this for real? Last year a friend of mine was killed by a bomb. These lunatics just don't give a hoot.

a) The presenter announced that a series of bomb hoaxes had thrown …

____

____

____

b) ______________________________

____

____

c) ____

____

d) ____

____

____

Aufgabe 8 **An Inaugural Address:** The following is an extract from President Woodrow Wilson's Inaugural Address[1] in 1913. He had been President of Princeton University and then became the Democratic candidate for the Presidency. Imagine you are reporting on the speech for a local newspaper. Turn the passage into indirect speech. Use as many different introductory verbs as possible.

"There has been a change of government. It began two years ago, when the House of Representatives became Democratic by a decisive majority. It has now been completed. The Senate about to assemble will also be democratic. The offices of President and Vice-President have been put into the hands of Democrats. What does that mean? That is the question that is uppermost in our minds today. That is the question I am going to try and answer, in order, if I may, to interpret the occasion.

It means much more than the mere success of a party. The success of a party means little except when the Nation is using that party for large and definite purpose. No one can mistake the purpose for which the nation now seeks to use the Democratic Party. It seeks to use it to interpret a change in its own plans and point of view. Some old things with which we had grown familiar, and which had begun to creep into the very habit of our thought and our lives, have altered their aspect as we have latterly looked critically upon them, with fresh, awakened eyes ..."

(From: Arthur S. Link et al., eds., The Papers of Woodrow Wilson, vol 27 1978, p. 148)

1 The speech a President makes after being sworn in.

The President began by saying that there had been a change of government.

Aufgabe 9 **Revision list:** Your task here is to simply fill in what the following words and phrases would normally change to after he/she said.

a) may → ______________________

b) can → ______________________

c) must (Notwendigkeit) → ______________________

d) must (Annahme) → ______________________

e) could → ______________________

f) might → ______________________

g) today → ______________________

h) yesterday → ______________________

i) last week → ______________________

j) now → ______________________

k) here → ______________________

l) this → ______________________

m) these → ______________________

n) my → ______________________

o) our → ______________________

p) last year → ______________________

q) two weeks ago → ______________________

r) I will go → ______________________

s) I am going → ______________________

Anhang

13 Schwierige Aufgaben zum Knobeln

Aufgabe 1 Your task is to translate the sentences into English.

a) Als er Kind war, wollte John Lehrer werden.
b) Darf ich bitte die Speisekarte sehen?
c) Mein Chef arbeitete drei Jahre lang als Koch in einem Hotel.
d) Seiner Meinung nach ist er der beste Lehrer in der Schule.
e) Das Gymnasium hat einen guten Ruf.
f) Wir haben eine neue Englischlehrerin bekommen.
g) Was bedeutet diese Frage?
h) Kinder haben eine wundervolle Phantasie.
i) Die Firma wurde 1987 gegründet.
j) Könntest du eine Tasse Tee für mich kochen?
k) Meine Haare sind viel zu lang.
l) Diese Marmalade schmeck toll.
m) Der Busfahrer hat unsere Buskarten kontrolliert.
n) Prüfen Sie bitte sein Ausweis.
o) Der Arzt hat ein Rezept geschrieben.
p) Die BBC hat gestern Abend eine sehr gute Sendung über Russland gesendet.
q) Kannst du mir dein Rezept für Irish Coffee geben?
r) Haben Sie die Karten zum Spiel bekommen?
s) Mein Büro muss jede Woche geputzt werden.

Aufgabe 2 Change the word in brackets so that the sentence is correct!

a) Denise (meet) ________________ your uncle last Friday.
b) Joan (break) ________________ four windows since she was born.
c) The last one she (shatter) ________________ was in the living-room.
d) (you – lock) ________________ the front door last night?
e) (you – get) ________________ many presents so far this year?
f) My shirts (shrink) ________________ in the wash we did yesterday.
g) How did you (cut) ________________ your finger?
h) Have you (set) ________________ the table?
i) I got a cold when I (lie) ________________ on the wet grass .
j) She skillfully (weave) ________________ a pattern on the handkerchief.

Aufgabe 3 Give the past and partciple forms of these verbs:

a) go ________________ ________________
b) teach ________________ ________________
c) buy ________________ ________________
d) ask ________________ ________________
e) write ________________ ________________
f) make ________________ ________________
g) fly ________________ ________________
h) know ________________ ________________

Aufgabe 4 **Cities of the world:** Some famous cities are hidden in these sentences. Find them and write the name of their country at the end of the line.

a) Well, on Don's birthday we all go to the seaside.
b) 'Below par' is a phrase used in golf.
c) When we are doing the washing tonight we must use new powder.
d) Are you going to give the money to Ron tomorrow?
e) When Mo scowlded at the policeman I knew we were in trouble.
f) In which year did James Douglas go west?
g) "A super throw from the England captain."

Aufgabe 5 **Wordgame:** Work on the following clues to discover a word that often means you have to use the *simple present.*

a) A letter you find at the end of the third person singular in the simple present.

b) go – went – ______________ (letter 2)

c) Gerry __________ows the lawn every weekend in summer. (letter 1)

d) Romeo to Juliet: I ______________________ you. (letter 4)

e) Ringo ______________, the drummer with the Beatles. (letter 2)

f) A document people entering the US must have. ____________ (letter 2)

g) What all immigrants hope to earn a lot of. __________________ (letter 1)

h) Old McDonald had a farm _ _ _ _ _ _ _ _ _ _ (letter 1)

i) The signal a ship sends when in trouble. __________________ (letter 1)

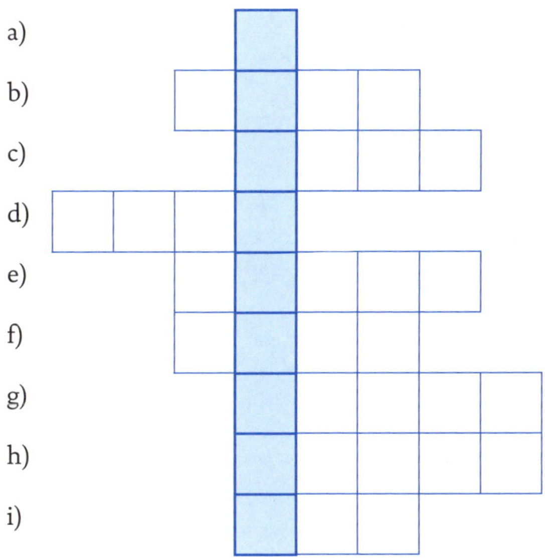

Aufgabe 6 Complete the words and say what grammatical form the word you have just filled in is!

a) A place by the roadside to walk on: _ _ _ _ _ _ _ _

b) Here you will find cars, or kitchens, or furniture to look at: _ _ _ _ _ _ _ _ _

c) He ran quickly _ _ _ _ _ _ the road.

d) Every day John ________ up at 7.30.

e) Another word for a place to walk on: _ _ _ _ _ _ _ _

f) I'm waiting ___ a bus.

g) I can play ____ guitar.

h) A person who owns something is the _ _ _ _ _

i) A person who doesn't want to work is _ _ _ _

j) I go to school ___ car.

k) John goes ___ foot.

l) If a person breaks my window I'm _ _ _ _ _

m) How do you say 'enttäuscht' ___ English?

n) He gives us tickets for wrong parking! _ _ _ _ _ _ _ _ _ _ _ _ _ _ _ _ .

14 Schwierige Wörter, die wir in diesem Buch benutzen

accomodation – Unterkunft
(to) acknowledge – anerkennen, zugeben, bestätigen
(to) adapt – sich anpassen
(to) admit – etwas zugeben
(to) advise – jemanden beraten
(to) advocate – befürworten
(to) allow – erlauben
(to) amass – anhäufen
ankle – Fußgelenk
(to) announce – ankündigen
(to) anticipate – erwarten, vorhersehen
(to) appreciate – schätzen
(to) approach – sich nähern
appropriate – passend
arrangements – Vereinbarung, Anordnung, Pläne
(to) arrest – festnehmen
artistry – Kunst
(to) assemble – zusammenbauen, sich versammeln
(to) assume – annehmen, ergreifen
attic – Speicher
audience – Publikum
asset – Liegenschaft
(to) assume – annehmen
attitude – Einstellung
(to) avoid – vermeiden
awkward – linkisch, ungeschickt

baggage – Gepäck
bank statement – Kontoauszug
barrel – Fass
(to) beg – betteln
behaviour – Verhalten
blacksmith – Hufschmied
bloodshed – Blutbad
(to) boast – angeben, prahlen
bomb hoax – falsche Bombendrohung
bough – Zweig

brackets	–	Klammern
brain disorders	–	Gehirnstörung
brand-new	–	nagelneu
(to) breeze in	–	schnell hereinkommen
briefing	–	Kurzinformation, Vorbereitung
(to) broaden	–	erweitern
candies	–	Süßigkeiten
(to) cascade	–	hinunterfließen
cataract	–	Katarakt (= Wasserfall, Stromschnelle)
(to) cater for	–	versorgen, eingestellt sein auf
cautiously	–	vorsichtig
chain	–	Kette
chat	–	plaudern
chilly	–	kühl
chiropodist	–	Orthopäde
circulation	–	Umlauf, Auflage (Zeitung)
chores	–	(unangenehme) Pflichten
clenched	–	geballt
(to) commission	–	in Auftrag geben
(to) compare	–	vergleichen
comprehensive	–	umfassend
(to) conceive	–	vorstellen, denken
(to) conduct	–	dirigieren, leiten
connections	–	Verbindungen
contemporary	–	Zeitgenosse
(to) contribute	–	beitragen
cranberry	–	Preiselbeere
crate	–	Kasten
(to) crouch	–	niederknien, sich bücken
curator	–	Kustos, Vormund
cute	–	süß, putzig
dear	–	teuer, liebe/lieber
debt	–	Schuld
demanding	–	anstrengend
(to) deny	–	ablehnen, verweigern
(to) describe	–	beschreiben
detached	–	freistehend (Haus)

(to) dispose of	–	loswerden, sich entledigen
dizzy	–	schwindlig
dotted line	–	punktierte Linie
drainpipe	–	Kanalisations-/Abflussrohr
(to) drape	–	drapieren
dreadful	–	schrecklich
drenched	–	durchnässt
dull	–	langweilig, trüb (Wetter)
editor	–	Redakteur
elaborate	–	kompliziert, gefeilt (Sprache)
(to) elapse	–	vergehen (Zeit)
(to) emphasize	–	betonen
(to) encourage	–	ermutigen
engaged	–	verlobt, besetzt
entitled	–	mit dem Titel
evil	–	schlecht
ewe	–	Mutterschaf
expedition	–	Forschungsreise
extension	–	Verlängerung, Anbau, Vergrößerung
fame	–	Ruhm
fence	–	Zaun
figure of speech	–	Stilfigur
filthy	–	sehr dreckig
first aid	–	Erste Hilfe
fitting	–	angemessen, passend
fittings	–	Zubehörteil, Ausstattung
flax	–	Flachs
(to) fling	–	werfen
(to) flock	–	in Scharen herbeikommen
folders	–	Aktenordner
(to) forecast	–	vorhersagen
former	–	ehemalig
forthcoming	–	bevorstehend
freelance	–	freiberuflich
frequently	–	häufig

gleam	–	Schein, Glanz
goods	–	Güter
goggles	–	Schutzbrille
gossip	–	Klatsch
guardian	–	Wächter
(to) gush	–	schnell herausfließen
headgear	–	Kopfschutz
hearse	–	Leichenwagen
hedge	–	Hecke
heir	–	Erbe
honour	–	Ehre
horrid	–	schrecklich
immediate	–	unmittelbar, sofort
income	–	Einkommen
inherent	–	innewohnend, eigen, inhärent
insignia	–	Insignien
introductory	–	einleitend
(to) intend	–	beabsichtigen
intolerable	–	unerträglich
item	–	Punkt, Sache
joint account	–	gemeinsames Bankkonto
jolly	–	fröhlich, jovial
latterly	–	in letzter Zeit
(to) launch	–	gründen, einführen, eröffnen
(to) limp	–	humpeln
linseed	–	Leinsamen
livestock	–	Vieh
loan	–	Darlehen
luggage	–	Gepäck
lumps	–	Klumpen
medals	–	Medaillen
(to) meet one's match	–	seinen Meister finden
memorial	–	Gedenktafel, Denkmal
(to) mention	–	erwähnen

mill	–	Mühle
misconceptions	–	falsche Vorstellungen
musket	–	Muskete (= Handfeuerwaffe)
(to) mutter	–	murmeln
momentous	–	bedeutsam
nailbiting	–	spannend
native	–	Ureinwohner
nightgown	–	Nachthemd
(to) nod (off)	–	einnicken, einschlafen
nursery	–	Kinderzimmer
(to) **o**bey	–	gehorchen
oblivious	–	vergesslich
(to have an) overdraft	–	Bankkonto überziehen
(to) overhaul	–	reparieren, überholen
palm	–	Handfläche
(to) pass away	–	sterben
passionately	–	leidenschaftlich
pitcher	–	Werfer
plug	–	Stecker
plumber	–	Klemptner
plummet	–	herunterstürzen
pools	–	Toto
popularity	–	Beliebtheit
(to) postpone	–	verschieben
(to) predict	–	voraussagen
prediction	–	Voraussage
previous	–	vorhergehend
privacy	–	Privatsphäre
proposal	–	Vorschlag
(to) psyche out	–	jdn. durchschauen
publication	–	Veröffentlichung
publishing house	–	Verlag
pumpkin	–	Kürbis
quarrel	–	Streit
quilt	–	Decke

ransom	–	Lösegeld
ratings	–	Zuschauerzahlen
realm	–	Bereich
recluse	–	Einsiedler
to refit	–	neu ausrüsten
to rely	–	ich auf jdn. verlassen
(to) remark	–	bemerken
renowned	–	berühmt
rented	–	gemietet
(to) replace	–	ersetzen
revival	–	Wiederaufblühen, Renaissence
roasted	–	gebraten
recognition	–	Anerkennung
(to) regret	–	bedauern
rejected	–	abgelehnt
(to) relate	–	sich beziehen auf
renowned	–	anerkannt, bekannt
replacement	–	Ersatz
reputation	–	Ruf
(to) retort	–	erwidern
(to) retreat	–	sich zurückziehen
revival	–	Wiedererwecken
rink	–	Bahn (Eislauf)
rope	–	Seil
(to) rouse	–	wecken
rubbish	–	Abfall
ruffians	–	Rüpel, Schläger

scalding	–	brühend heiß
scarce	–	knapp
scuttle	–	Kohleneimer
semi-detatched	–	Doppelhaushälfte
settler	–	Siedler
shareholder	–	Aktionär
(to) shatter	–	zerschmettern
shepherd	–	Schäfer
silken	–	seidig
site	–	Anwesen, Grundstück
sledge	–	Schlitten

(to) sob – schluchzen, weinen
sore – weh tun
sound effects – Klangeffekte
(to) spin – sich drehen
(to go for a) spin – eine Fahrt machen
splint – Schiene
spoilsport – Spielverderber
staff – Stab
stall – Stand
(to) stir – rühren
stranded – festsitzen, auf dem Trockenen sitzen
sublime – erhaben, überragend
(to) submit – vorlegen, einreichen
(to) succeed – Erfolg haben
superficial – oberflächlich
(to) surprise – überraschen
survey – Überblick, Umfrage

tedious – langweilig, anstrengend
tenement – Mietshaus
(to) threaten – drohen
tip – Spitze
trade fair – Messe
tramworker – Straßenbahnarbeiter
tummy – Bauch
(to) twist an ankle – sich den Fuß vertreten

uppermost – oberste

vague – unbestimmt
value – Wert
vendor – Verkäufer
venison – Wild (Fleisch)
vintage car – Oldtimer

(to) wade – waten
(to) whine – winseln
wing – Flügel
wireless – Radio

15 Unregelmäßige Verben

Infinitiv	Präteritum	Partizip Perfekt	deutsche Übersetzung
be	was	been	*sein*
bear	bore	born(e)	*(er)tragen; gebären*
beat	beat	beaten	*schlagen*
become	became	become	*werden*
begin	began	begun	*beginnen*
bet	bet	bet	*wetten*
bind	bound	bound	*binden*
bite	bit	bit(ten)	*beißen*
bleed	bled	bled	*bluten*
blow	blew	blown	*blasen*
break	broke	broken	*brechen*
bring	brought	brought	*bringen*
broadcast	broadcast	broadcast	*senden*
build	built	built	*bauen*
burn	burnt/ed	burnt/ed	*brennen*
burst	burst	burst	*platzen*
buy	bought	bought	*kaufen*
catch	caught	caught	*fangen*
choose	chose	chosen	*wählen*
come	came	come	*kommen*
cost	cost	cost	*kosten*
creep	crept	crept	*kriechen*
cut	cut	cut	*schneiden*
deal	dealt	dealt	*handeln*
dig	dug	dug	*graben*
do	did	done	*tun*
draw	drew	drawn	*zeichnen, ziehen*
dream	dreamt/ed	dreamt/ed	*träumen*
drink	drank	drunk	*trinken*
drive	drove	driven	*fahren*
eat	ate	eaten	*essen*
fall	fell	fallen	*fallen*
feed	fed	fed	*füttern*
feel	felt	felt	*fühlen*
fight	fought	fought	*kämpfen*
find	found	found	*finden*

Infinitiv	Präteritum	Partizip Perfekt	deutsche Übersetzung
flee	fled	fled	*fliehen*
fling	flung	flung	*schleudern, werfen*
fly	flew	flown	*fliegen*
forbid	forbade	forbidden	*verbieten*
forget	forgot	forgotten	*vergessen*
forgive	forgave	forgiven	*vergeben*
freeze	froze	frozen	*frieren*
get	got	got	*bekommen*
give	gave	given	*geben*
go	went	gone	*gehen*
grow	grew	grown	*wachsen*
hang	hung	hung	*hängen*
have	had	had	*haben*
hear	heard	heard	*hören*
hide	hid	hidden	*verstecken*
hit	hit	hit	*treffen, schlagen*
hold	held	held	*halten*
hurt	hurt	hurt	*verletzen*
keep	kept	kept	*halten*
know	knew	known	*wissen*
lay	laid	laid	*legen*
lead	led	led	*leiten*
learn	learnt/ed	learnt/ed	*lernen*
leave	left	left	*lassen*
lend	lent	lent	*leihen*
lean	leant/ed	leant/ed	*lehnen*
let	let	let	*lassen*
lie	lay	lain	*liegen*
light	lit/ed	lit/ed	*beleuchten*
lose	lost	lost	*verlieren*
make	made	made	*machen*
mean	meant	meant	*meinen, bedeuten*
meet	met	met	*treffen*
pay	paid	paid	*bezahlen*
put	put	put	*setzen, stellen, legen*
read	read	read	*lesen*
ride	rode	ridden	*fahren, reiten*
ring	rang	rung	*läuten*

Infinitiv	Präteritum	Partizip Perfekt	deutsche Übersetzung
rise	rose	risen	*aufstehen, aufgehen*
run	ran	run	*laufen, rennen*
say	said	said	*sagen*
see	saw	seen	*sehen*
seek	sought	sought	*suchen*
sell	sold	sold	*verkaufen*
send	sent	sent	*senden*
set	set	set	*setzen, stellen*
sew	sewed	sown	*nähen*
shake	shook	shaken	*schütteln*
shine	shone	shone	*scheinen*
shoot	shot	shot	*schießen*
show	showed	shown	*zeigen*
shrink	shrank	shrunk	*schrumpfen, einlaufen*
shut	shut	shut	*schließen*
sing	sang	sung	*singen*
sink	sank	sunk	*sinken*
sit	sat	sat	*sitzen*
sleep	slept	slept	*schlafen*
slide	slid	slid	*gleiten*
smell	smelt	smelt	*riechen*
speak	spoke	spoken	*sprechen*
speed	sped	sped	*sich beeilen, beschleunigen*
spell	spelt	spelt	*buchstabieren*
spend	spent	spent	*verbringen, ausgeben*
spill	spilt/ed	spilt/ed	*verschütten*
split	split	split	*spalten, teilen*
spoil	spoilt/ed	spoilt/ed	*verderben*
spread	spread	spread	*ausbreiten*
spring	sprang	sprung	*springen*
stand	stood	stood	*stehen*
steal	stole	stolen	*stehlen*
stick	stuck	stuck	*kleben*
strike	struck	struck	*stoßen, schlagen*
stink	stank	stunk	*stinken*
swear	swore	sworn	*fluchen; schwören*
sweep	swept	swept	*fegen*
swim	swam	swum	*schwimmen*

Infinitiv	Präteritum	Partizip Perfekt	deutsche Übersetzung
swing	swung	swung	*schwingen*
take	took	taken	*nehmen*
teach	taught	taught	*lehren*
tear	tore	torn	*reißen*
tell	told	told	*erzählen*
think	thought	thought	*denken, glauben*
throw	threw	thrown	*werfen*
understand	understood	understood	*verstehen*
wake	woke	woken	*aufwachen, wecken*
wear	wore	worn	*tragen*
weave	wove	woven	*weben*
weep	wept	wept	*weinen*
win	won	won	*gewinnen*
write	wrote	written	*schreiben*

Lösungen

1 Präpositionen

Aufgabe 1

a) in, at
b) through, above
c) behind
d) on top of
e) beside, in

Aufgabe 2

at/by, on, from/off/on, in, into, in, to, into, on, towards/into, beside, in, above/over, by, towards/to/at, in

Aufgabe 3

a) at
b) in
c) at
d) for
e) during
f) after
g) in
h) before
i) by
j) until/before
k) while
l) by
m) at
n) on
o) on
p) in
q) at

Aufgabe 4

- How long have you been living in France?
- I've been living/have lived in France since 1980 and in Paris itself for 4 years.
- I have been learning French for a long time.
- Well I have been attending a first aid course since Christmas and I have been learning to dance for the past six months.
- Have you seen any good plays lately?
- No I haven't attended the theatre this year.
- I've worked/I've been working in my present school since 1994.
- Oh yes I've been trying to get a job in England for ages.

Aufgabe 5

a) on fire
b) on strike
c) to lunch
d) in cash
e) by cheque
f) in love

Aufgabe 6

(1) dreamt of, (2) got interested in, (3) depart for, (4) arrive at, (5) deal with, (6) careless about, (7) feel sorry for, (8) get angry at, (9) laugh at, (10) good at, (11) apologize for, (12) learn from

Aufgabe 7

to get on to, to cut down, to look for, to cut off, to pick up, to look after, to pick out, to turn down, to blow up, to turn into, to give out to, to put out, to blow out, to give away, to put on, to get off

Aufgabe 8

(1) on, (2) at, (3) at, (4) for, (5) on, (6) with, (7) out of, (8) of, (9) for, (10) to, (11) past, (12) between, (13) by, (14) on, (15) of, (16) with, (17) at, (18) behind, (19) to, (20) in, (21) for, (22) on, (23) of, (24) for, (25) of, (26) for, (27) at/by, (28) into, (29) into, (30) on/at, (31) into, (32) through, (33) from/of

Aufgabe 9

a) at, on, of
b) in
c) for
d) at
e) by, in
f) in
g) by
h) in
i) of
j) down
k) for
l) until
m) after, in
n) in
o) for
p) outside
q) for
r) in
s) to
t) to
u) by
v) in
w) of
x) at
y) to
z) of

Aufgabe 10 Hi Tom,

Thanks a million for your mail. The photo of your school looked really good. What kind of camera have you? I must say I am a bit jealous of the new building you have moved into. That looks like a great basketball court. Do you play a lot of basketball? Here in Munich things are much the same as they always were. I got into a lot of trouble lately with my English teacher. He's really old and doesn't like students whose English is as good as his. I told him that I heard people say loads of things in England which are not in our textbook!! We have school tests all next week and I am really worried about the Maths test. I hate maths and our teacher explains things once and once only. So if you miss it the first time then you've had it I'm afraid. Have you any plans for your summer hols? Why don't you come to Munich in July and you could come to school with me in the morning. Then we could go play football in the afternoon. It would be great. I have just started learning how to play the guitar so maybe I'll teach you a few things. Why don't you ask your parents if they would let you travel to Germany on your own. Perhaps we could then travel back to England for a week or two in August. Let me know what you think of this idea. Say hello to all your family for me.

Regards,
Franz

2 Adjektive

Aufgabe 1 counterpart: a person or thing which corresponds to or has the same function as s.b./sth.
cute: attractive
tedious: boring
evil: bad
rating: ranking, classification
stunt: a feat of daring or skill
superficial: not deep, relating to the surface

Aufgabe 2

- a nice young girl
- a cute blue-eyed baby
- an angry middle-aged man
- an ugly tattered teddy bear

- a gorgeous, dark-haired princess
- a horrid black spider
- filthy grey socks
- a beautiful well-known Irish song
- a tedious, badly-written first novel
- an unattractive, expensive ring

Aufgabe 3

a) Is your English teacher English or American?
b) The rich often keep to themselves.
c) For the blind, life without help is difficult.
d) The French like to sing and dance.
e) In the animal kingdom the strong eat the weak.
f) The young are often impatient with the old.
g) The Dutch are a world power in football.
h) In special/certain schools the deaf can learn how to make themselves understood.
i) The good in people often goes unrecognized.
j) The disabled are often not well enough looked after.
k) The Indians honoured their dead in song and in story.

Aufgabe 4

to admit	zugeben	admissible	admittance/admission
to allow	erlauben	allowable	allowance
to avoid	vermeiden	avoidable	avoidance
to believe	glauben	believable	belief
to blind	blenden	blinding	blindness
to depart	abfahren	departing	departure
to describe	beschreiben	descriptive	description
to die	sterben	dying/dead	death
to demand	verlangen	demanding	demand
to enjoy	geniessen	enjoyable	enjoyment
to escape	flüchten	escaping	escape
to free	befreien	free	freedom
to harm	schaden	harmful	harm
to include	einschließen	inclusive	inclusion
to persuade	überreden	persuasive	persuasion
to revolt	rebellieren	revolting	revolution
to sell	verkaufen	saleable	sale
to succeed	gelingen	successful	success

to surprise	überraschen	surprising	surprise
to taste	schmecken	tasty	taste
to understand	verstehen	understandable	understanding

Aufgabe 5

a) excited, exciting
b) terrified, terrifying
c) amazed, amazing
d) tired, tiring
e) depressed, depressing
f) confusing, confused
g) bored, boring

Aufgabe 6

List A

dark, darker, darkest
brainy, brainier, brainiest
impossible, more/most impossible
wonderful, more/most wonderful
clever, cleverer, cleverest
busy, busier, busiest
stale, staler, stalest
early, earlier, earliest
useful, more/most useful
doubtful, more/most doubtful
frightening, more/most frightening
tall, taller, tallest
beautiful, more/most beautiful
far, farther, farthest
gorgeous, more/most gorgeous
scarce, scarcer, scarcest
loud, louder, loudest
rough, rougher, roughest

List B

fast, faster, fastest
dreamy, dreamier, dreamiest
severe more/most severe
hopeful, more/most hopeful
sincere, more/most sincere
merry, merrier, merriest
late, later, latest
idle, more/most idle
new, newer, newest
pretty, prettier, prettiest
obscure, more/most obscure
careful, more/most careful
suitable, more/most suitable
tender, more/most tender
intelligent, more/most intelligent
plentiful, more/most plentiful
noisy, noisier, noisiest
far, further, furthest

Aufgabe 7

(1) longer than, (2) earlier than, (3) livelier, (4) more expensive than, (5) better, (6) more, (7) than, (8) more famous, (9) better than, (10) worse than, (11) better, (12) more interesting, (13) more satisfying than, (14) shorter, (15) more superficial

Aufgabe 8
a) best
b) most interesting
c) most elegant
d) tastier than
e) most inspiring
f) most disappointing
g) sweetest

3 Adverbien

Aufgabe 1
a) miserably
b) extremely
c) sublimely
d) happily
e) mercifully
f) intolerably

Aufgabe 2
(1) fairly, (2) skilfully, (3) cautiously, (4) cruelly, (5) angrily, (6) comfortably, (7) regularly, (8) finally (note: not *lastly* which means something different), (9) cruelly

Aufgabe 3
a) Conversation still plays an important part in daily life here./ Conversation plays an important part in daily life here still.
b) A woman has never been Prime Minister of this country.
c) One particular woman, Maire Geoghegan-Quinn, has just retired from politics after twenty years service.
d) The country is currently enjoying an increased standard of living thanks to tourism and EC membership./ The country is enjoying an increased standard of living currently thanks to tourism and EC membership.
e) The country rarely wins major sporting events./ The country wins major sporting events rarely.
f) Farming remains vitally important in this land.
g) The people enjoy traditional sports such as hurling very much.
h) In 2003 people flocked to the cinemas to see a film about Veronica Guerin.
i) Radio talkshows such as Marion Finucane's Liveline are immensely popular there.
j) In 2003, Eoin Colfer's third 'Artemis Fowl' book was well received by the critics.
k) Aer Lingus, the national airline, regularly flies people to and from Germany./

Aer Lingus, the national airline, flies people to and from Germany regularly.

l) This ultra-Catholic nation finally voted in favour of divorce in 1995.
Name of the country: The Republic of Ireland

Aufgabe 4

a) This movie has often been called a blockbuster of a film.
b) It was brilliantly directed by Steven Spielberg./
It was directed brilliantly by Steven Spielberg.
c) It was conceived by George Lucas in the 1970s.
d) The music for the film was carefully composed by John Williams./
The music for the film was composed carefully by John Williams.
e) Karen Allen plays the leading lady beautifully in the film./
Karen Allen plays the leading lady in the film beautifully.
f) The storyline develops quickly and centres around a freelance treasure hunter who is searching desperately for something. (Note: both could go before the verb as well)
g) Harrison Ford performs powerfully as the main character.
h) The sequel to this film was equally dramatic and was called Indiana Jones and the Temple of Doom.

Name of the film: Raiders of The Lost Ark

Aufgabe 5

a)	early	early	earlier	earliest
b)	safe	safely	more safely	most safely
c)	intensive	intensively	more intensively	most intensively
d)	sure	surely	more surely	most surely
e)	fortunate	fortunately	more fortunately	most fortunately
f)	sensible	sensibly	more sensibly	most sensibly
g)	high	highly	more highly	most highly
h)	deserved	deservedly	more deservedly	most deservedly
i)	jolly	in a jolly way	in a jollier way	in the jolliest way
j)	similiar	similiarly	more similiarly	most similiarly
k)	true	truly	more truly	most truly
l)	deep	deeply	more deeply	most deeply
m)	whole	wholly	— —	

Aufgabe 6 (1) worse, (2) better, (3) hardest, (4) later, (5) badly, (6) more beautifully, (7) most energetically, (8) highly

Aufgabe 7 (1) more cheaply, (2) more carefully and beautifully than, (3) most efficiently, (4) most delightfully, (5) harder than, (6) faster, (7) earlier than, (8) most warmly, (9) more quickly than, (10) more clearly, (11) most significantly, (12) older, (13) more famous, (14) continuously

Aufgabe 8 popular, well-produced, large, awful, tired, new, sad, confident, gripping, famous, single, early, incredible, entire, straight, difficult

Aufgabe 9 (1) lately, (2) closely, (3) hardly, (4) last, (5) badly, (6) bad, (7) dearly, (8) simply, (9) dear, (10) just, (11) fairly, (12) justly, (13) close, (14) highly, (15) high, (16) shortly, (17) short, (18) closely, (19) express, (20) expressly, (21) wary

Aufgabe 10 (1) properly, (2) foolishly, (3) well/wisely, (4) home-based, (5) regularly, (6) terrible, (7) incredibly, (8) monthly, (9) probably, (10) completely, (11) angry, (12) instantly, (13) carefully, (14) good/serious, (15) badly, (16) friendly, (17) expensive, (18) seriously, (19) closely, (20) wisely, (21) faster, (22) happy

Aufgabe 11 green – adjective, plenty – adjective, early – adverb, wrong – adjective, gently – adverb, after – preposition, quite – adverb, dark – noun, dead – noun, dark – adjective, beside – preposition, silent – adjective, chilly – adjective, alone – adverb

Aufgabe 12 I recall the morning I got up and went to the back door for a breath of fresh air. There was this cute little dog lying there all cold and tired looking. He took me completely by surprise. I bent slowly down and patted him and could clearly see he was lost and weak. I called my daughter Tara who was still fast asleep in bed. She didn't know what was going on but she soon came to life when she saw the cute dog. "What will we do with him?" I asked her. "Bring him in and give him breakfast" she smiled, lifting the dog into her arms. We gave him food and water and before long he was a member of our family. That was really nice because we had just moved to a town north of Dublin and didn't know a soul. We called him "Paddy" and set about trying to find his real home. We had no luck despite putting an ad in the paper so we then decided to keep him. Having a dog in the house has changed everything for us. Tara loves minding him and when I'm on my own I still have somebody to talk to. It's great to have a dog as he is good against burglars. Likewise, Paddy has to be taken out for a walk every morning and evening which is a healthy way of keeping fit. I wouldn't part with him for all the the world. Sometimes I ask myself what kind of owner didn't want to keep him but I'm so glad of that because otherwise we would never have met him. My dog means the world to me.

4 Zeitformen des Verbs

Aufgabe 1

a) Money makes the world go round.
b) All roads lead to Rome
c) What goes up must come down.
d) The early bird catches the worm.

Aufgabe 2

People have to get up at 8 o'clock. How lucky they are! They eat breakfast at around 8.20. Helen eats two eggs and sausages every morning of the week. No wonder she's fat! People over here stand in a straight line when waiting for a bus. They throw all their rubbish into the one bin. I wonder who sorts it all out. The English drink tea all day long it seems to me. Of course the strangest thing of all is that they drive on the left-hand side of the road. I needn't tell you it rains a lot here. There hasn't been one dry day since I arrived. I should have brought my boots! See you soon.

Aufgabe 3

a) … is chasing the dog.
b) Tom is carrying things.
c) Lucy is listening to loud music.
d) Catherine is reading her German schoolbook.
e) Grandad is singing Lili Marlene and playing the guitar.
f) Mrs Fishburn is lying on the bed.

Aufgabe 4

a) leaves
b) are boarding
c) to give, to store, greets
d) read, eat, sleep, has
e) are listening
f) stops, checks

Aufgabe 5

a) I was born in Brookline, USA in 1917.
b) In 1940 I graduated from Harvard University.
c) In 1940 I wrote the book "Why England Slept".
d) In 1941 I joined the navy and fought in World War II.
e) In 1946 I ran for Congress.
f) In 1953 I married Jackie.
g) In 1960 I beat Richard Nixon.
h) In 1963 I died in my wife's arms.

My name: John F. Kennedy

Aufgabe 6

went, bought, put, sat, watched, took, slipped, went, bought, kept, kissed, thanked, let

Aufgabe 7

a) The moment the train stopped I was drying my hair.
b) The moment the train stopped we were trying to close a suitcase.
c) The moment the train stopped I was lying on the seat reading a book.
d) The moment the train stopped I was thinking of home.
e) The moment the train stopped I was putting a stamp on a letter.
f) The moment the train stopped I was tying my shoelace.
g) The moment the train stopped I was writing a letter to a friend.
h) The moment the train stopped I was taking photographs of the countryside.
i) The moment the train stopped I was peeling/eating an orange.

Aufgabe 8

Our car has broken down and my Dad has been trying to fix it. Grandad, believe it or not has fallen in love and Tom has bought a new radio cassette recorder. Mammy has caught a cold and has taken to her bed. I have read five books since we got here because it has been raining cats and dogs for the past two weeks. We have all started to get on each others nerves. I have learned a good deal of German but thank God the hols will soon be over. See you Friday. Love, ...

Aufgabe 9
a) walked, have been, Britain
b) have stood, have visited, Australia
c) have watched, have attended, US
d) have swum, have spent, Canada
e) have slept, have seen, Italy

Aufgabe 10
a) have been working
b) have you been learning
c) has been sleeping
d) have been spending
e) have been lying

Aufgabe 11
(1) has been, (2) has attracted, (3) came, (4) have tried, (5) have survived, (6) was, (7) went, (8) remains, (9) come, (10) amazed, (11) is, (12) boasts, (13) cut, (14) provide, (15) has always had, (16) described, (17) makes, (18) wished, (19) is, (20) do, (21) fish, (22) hunt, (23) relax, (24) has grown, (25) celebrated, (26) seems, (27) to have been, (28) lasted, (29) visit, (30) to hear, (31) know, (32) had, (33) echoes

Aufgabe 12
asset: anything valuable or useful
to boast: to be excessively proud of sth. when speaking
musket: a form of gun
a barrel: a wooden container for holding water, apples etc.
to retreat: to withdraw in the face of military opposition
renowned: famous

Aufgabe 13
a) had read
b) had done
c) had eaten
d) had explained
e) had returned
f) had given
g) had sat

Aufgabe 14
a) had served, became
b) set foot
c) was, decided, had left
d) had passed, climbed
e) had examined, came, questioned
f) had been, had paid, had worked, had learnt
g) had given, headed off

Aufgabe 15

Secretary: Breakfast will take roughly an hour
Journalist: What will the P.M. do after breakfast?
Secretary: He is doing an interview with the Times at 10.00
Journalist: What comes after that?
Secretary: He is taking a call from the US ambassador at 11.00
Journalist: What will he then do?
Secretary: At 11.30 a car will arrive to take him to Heathrow to catch his flight to Belfast.
Journalist: What time is his flight scheduled to leave?
Secretary: He will leave at 12.30, all being well.
Journalist: What time will he be meeting the N.I. Conservative Party?
Secretary: At 2.00
Journalist: Do you know what time he'll arrive back in London?
Secretary: He will return at 4.30. and should be here some time after 5.30. At 6.00 he will meet his wife and family for tea and he is attending the opening of King Lear at 8.00. Any further questions?
Journalist: Yes. What time will he be home at?
Secretary: Sometime around midnight.

Aufgabe 16

- had decided: past perfect. It is used here because she decided this before leaving.
- have always been: present perfect
- loves: present simple
- left: past simple
- did I know: past simple. Used to describe something in the past and an example of inversion.
- would: conditional. Something that would one day happen.
- was working: past continuous
- had just married: past perfect
- used to tell: past simple. Used to describe something she always did out of habit in the past.
- had been asking: past perfect continuous
- they'll go: future tense. Used to express future event.
- happens: present simple. Used to express future
- remember: present simple

Aufgabe 17 Check pages 168–172

Aufgabe 18 After the immigrants had finished the interviews and health examinations, these would-be Americans travelled on to New York and other cities. However, a small minority ended up in a room on Ellis Island from where they were deported. Their futures depended so much on what happened that day that for many it was an experience they never forgot. From 1924 on, after Congress had passed a new law, the island was no longer used as an immigration centre.

In 1990 Ellis Island opened once again but this time as a museum. Already millions of Americans have visited the centre and have relived their ancestors' first steps in the New World. There have been many other famous immigration centres in the history of the United States (Angel Island for instance in San Francisco also became famous) but it is doubtful if any of them will ever be as well known as Ellis Island.

Aufgabe 19 New Year's Eve in Glasgow

The Royal Concert Hall in Glasgow was the venue for this year's Hogmanay Gala and a huge crowd turned up to witness the event. Our well-known presenter Una McLean did a splendid job and helped make everyone feel at home for this musical feast. The music was superbly played by the Royal Scottish National Orchestra. The orchestra was conducted by Richard Balcombe. While I was listening to the music I could see people getting into great form. The Scottish songs got a huge response from the audience. If anyone had been in a bad mood coming here then their dark clouds were quickly blown away by the likes of Bizet, Rossini and Mendelssohn. It will take a really good concert next year to beat this one but should the wonderful singer Clare Shearer be taking part again, it may surpass the quality experienced by the large crowd here the other night. We'll have to wait and see.

5 Passiv

Aufgabe 1 was built: simple past
named: simple past
had been formed: past perfect
(had been) rented: past perfect
was being constructed: past progressive
had been amassed: past perfect
is overshadowed: present simple

are found: present simple
has been left unpainted: present perfect
was covered: past simple
being painted: past progressive
has been described: present perfect
was purchased: past simple
had been evacuated: past perfect
has been refitted: present perfect
are being conducted: present progressive
it is hoped: simple present
will be completed: future

Aufgabe 2 (1) was used, (2) were placed, (3) was discussed, (4) was founded, (5) were submitted, (6) were accepted, (7) was authorized, (8) was being constructed, (9) was passed, (10) was undertaken, (11) were developed, (12) completed

Aufgabe 3
a) In 1494 the country was claimed for Spain by Christopher Columbus.
b) In 1655 this country was captured from Spain by the English.
c) Over two hundred native species of orchids are grown by this country.
d) (Their) votes were cast by the people for the first time shortly after the Second World War.
e) English and a dialect called patois are spoken by the inhabitants.
f) A traditional dress consisting of a long skirt and a headdress made out of bandana are worn by the women.
g) To earn a living the land is farmed by the people.
h) The many tourists who come every year are also catered for by them.
i) In 1720 the people were led by Nanny of the Maroons in a war against the British.
j) World fastest times for the 100 and 200 metres were run by Merlene Ottey in the 1980s and 1990s.

The name of this country is Jamaica.

Aufgabe 4
a) ... has been rebuilt by the new owners.
b) ... has been put in by the new owners.
c) ... has been rehung by the new owners.

d) … has been erected by the new owners.
e) … has been fixed by the new owners.
f) … have been made by the new owners.
g) … has been inserted by the new owners.
h) … have been planted by the new owners.
i) … has been tidied up by the new owners.
j) … has been bought by the new owners.

Aufgabe 5
a) Preparations for Thanksgiving would normally be started days beforehand (by Americans).
b) Differences in the Thanksgiving menu will be found from family to family.
c) Sweet potatoes, onions, green peas, cranberry sauce, nuts, fruit and candies would be included in a Thanksgiving shopping list.
d) Usually pies will be baked by the person preparing the feast.
e) Greeting cards would also be bought and made by families.
f) The turkey would be seen as the centrepiece of the meal by all Americans.
g) The great bird will be filled with all sorts of delicious stuffing by the cook.
h) A special place will be reserved for the turkey on the Thanksgiving dinner table by Americans for years to come.
i) A lot of work will have been put in by the parents by the time the feast comes round.
j) Wild turkey would have been eaten roasted over an open fire at the first Pilgrims' thanksgiving feast.
k) Fish and venison would also have been enjoyed by them.
l) Corn buried in sand would have been found by the first pilgrims.
m) Ears of corn will often be hung up as decorations by a family celebrating Thanksgiving.
n) Pumpkins will be eaten by many people next Thanksgiving because it is said pumpkins were eaten by the original pilgrims.

Aufgabe 6
a) The woman is hanging up the washing.
The washing is being hung up by the woman.
b) The woman is baking a cake.
A cake is being baked by the woman.
c) The woman is watering the plants.
The plants are being watered by the woman.

d) The woman is using the hoover.
The hoover is being used by the woman.
e) The man is reading the paper.
The paper is being read by the man.
f) The man is asking a question.
A question is being asked by the man.
g) Somebody is making a phonecall.
A phonecall is being made by somebody.
h) The man is smoking a cigarette.
A cigarette is being smoked by the man.
i) The man is doing absolutely nothing.
Absolutely nothing is being done by the man.
j) The woman is doing all the jobs.
All the jobs are being done by the woman.

Aufgabe 7

a) A newspaper was bought by Will Rogers for his children nearly every day.
Will Roger's children were bought a newspaper nearly every day.
b) The young Will Rogers was given a job as a cattle hand by an American cattle farmer.
A job as a cattle hand was given to the young Will Rogers by an American cattle farmer.
c) Soon he was offered a position as an entertainer by the owner of a Wild West show.
A position as an entertainer was offered to him by the owner of a Wild West show.
d) Will was promised more money by the man if he was good.
More money was promised to Will by the man if he was good.
e) The visitors were often taught simple rope tricks by Will.
Simple rope tricks were often taught to the visitors by Will.
f) The people were also told good jokes that he had read in newspapers.
Good jokes that he had read in newspapers were also told to the people.
g) His girl Betty was bought a wedding ring by Will in 1908.
A wedding ring was bought for his girl Betty in 1908.
h) She was promised a good and happy life by him.
A good and happy life was promised to her by him.
i) Will Rogers was given a fitting funeral by America when he died in 1935.
A fitting funeral was given to Will Rogers by America when he died in 1935.

Aufgabe 8 In the 1950s an important decision was arrived at by the people of the Blasket Islands, a group of islands off the west coast of Ireland. A government proposal to leave the islands and accept land on the mainland in return was agreed to by them. The proposals had been thought about carefully beforehand by them. Irish was spoken by the islanders and land and sea relied upon to stay alive. After the Great War the numbers of fish that were being caught by the people grew smaller. Financial support from sons and daughters in America was now relied on by them to stay alive. Every winter the poverty of their hard lives was dealt with by them as best they could. The resettlement proposals were heard about and discussed by them. The idea was laughed at at first by one or two islanders. The proposals were listened to by most of the people however. The government was asked for help by them. Eventually, in 1953, the people were taken off the island by officials.

Aufgabe 9
a) ... the M.P. should resign.
b) ... the M.P. is guilty of a number of offences.
c) ... he will offer his resignation.
d) ... he should not be given another job in Whitehall.
e) ... he did not deliberately mislead parliament.
f) ... he will no longer be part of the political scene.
g) ... he has been an M.P. for 46 years.
h) ... he would have made a good Foreign Minister.
i) ... M.P.s never err.
j) ... he will now concentrate on writing his memoirs.

Aufgabe 10 A European motorway speed limit of 120 km per hour would be a good thing. It is fully accepted by experts on both sides of this discussion that far too many people die on our roads. It is taken for granted by many that this is just an unfortunate consequence of the huge numbers of cars on our roads. It is to be regretted that people continue to believe this when in fact it is irresponsible driving, and in particular speeding, which is the most frequent cause of death on our roads. It is thought a European limit of 120 km per hour would help save many lives. It is widely hoped by many that improved roads and safer cars will reduce the numbers injured and killed every year. I don't agree. Until drivers begin to take full responsibility for their actions on the road people will continue to die needlessly all over Europe. I am therefore in favour of the motion in hand and believe that the sooner it is introduced the better.

Aufgabe 11 The National Army Museum is located in Chelsea, London. The museum was established in 1960 and since then materials relating to the British Army have been steadily collected and put on exhibition. Two of the galleries present in the museum are devoted to a chronological survey of the Army. Weapons and medals are housed in the Uniform Gallery and the development of hand weapons is traced in the Weapon Gallery.
Enquiries should be sent to The Curator, National Army Museum, Royal Hospital Road, Chelsea. Mr Bottomley is to be contacted by anyone seeking guided tours and the museum may be visited from 10.00 to 5.30 Monday to Saturday and on a Sunday from 2.00 to 5.30. A new wing is being built at the moment and it is hoped to carry out further extensions in 2002. This is a museum which would really have been appreciated by the Duke of Wellington.

6 Modale Hilfsverben

Aufgabe 1
a) It might not work out.
b) May I borrow your pen?
c) May I open the window?
d) I'm afraid I might fail.
e) I might not get a visa.
f) May I have the butter please?
g) May I have some information about the trade fair?
h) May I turn the radio up?

Aufgabe 2
a) I must water them then.
b) must, needn't, needs
c) mustn't
d) must cut
e) needn't
f) mustn't drive faster
g) You must get new ones …
h) You must go on a diet.

Aufgabe 3 must, may, needn't, may, must, mustn't, mustn't, must, must, needn't, must, may, may

Aufgabe 4

a) You should eat more!
b) Shall I help you carry your bags?
c) You shouldn't eat so much.
d) Shall I show you how to find a book?
e) You shouldn't drive so fast!
f) Shall I show you how to dance?
g) You shouldn't smoke so much!

Aufgabe 5

a) Will/Shall I give Anita a present.
b) Such incomes shouldn't be allowed.
c) She should rather stay.
d) Jane shouldn't sell the car too cheaply.
e) My father shouldn't have given her the car as a present.
f) Jim is said to have sold his house.
g) The delivery is to be carried out very quickly.
h) You're to clear up the sitting-room immediately.

Aufgabe 6

a) ... could play basketball.
... be able to play basketball.
b) ... he couldn't speak English.
... he won't be able to speak English.
c) ... they couldn't ski very well.
... they won't be able to ski very well.
d) ... she couldn't swim ...
... she will be able to swim.

Aufgabe 7

a) My parents have said I may go on holidays with my friends in the summer.
I wasn't allowed to go on holidays with my friends. My family was too poor.
b) My parents have said I must/I will have to study hard if I want to pass my exams.
I didn't have to study hard. We did no exams.
c) I can do my driving test at the age of eighteen.
I couldn't do my test because there were no cars around.
d) We have to dispose of of our rubbish carefully.
We didn't have to dispose of our rubbish carefully in those days.
e) My parents say I may go to a disco once a week.
My parents didn't allow me to go to dances.

f) I can fly to any part of the world.
I couldn't fly! There were no planes.

g) I will have to get a job and start a career after school.
I didn't have to get a job after school. I had to stay at home.

Aufgabe 8

a) The shepherd won't have to look after his sheep ...
b) ... he didn't have to tend to a limping ewe's sore foot.
c) ... won't have a new lot of sheep to care for.
d) ... the shepherd's dog didn't have to work hard.
e) The dog needn't run quickly in order to catch the sheep ...
f) ... can't whistle very well ...
g) The shepherd doesn't have to take shelter ...

Aufgabe 9

a) can
b) might / will / may
c) can
d) should
e) may / must
f) have to
g) will have to / should
h) would / might
i) will / should
j) needn't

Aufgabe 10

a) They ought to be ashamed of it.
b) She must accept things as they are and make the best of them.
c) And we ought not and we cannot and we must not wait another 8 months before we get a bill.
d) Should I register as a Democrat?
e) She was to meet the Bible salesman at ten o'clock.
f) I'll have to send a wire to Portland.
g) We should not have sent Tom to Chicago.
h) Dad said he had to do this too when he was little / small.

7 Infinitiv

Aufgabe 1

a) to wake
b) to be sad about something especially something said or done
c) horrible
d) from the start
e) rushed

Aufgabe 2

(1) to dream, (2) to wake, (3) to rouse, (4) to work, (5) to finish, (6) to show, (7) to read, (8) to listen, (9) to argue, (10) to throw, (11) to rescue, (12) to regret, (13) to like, (14) to publish

The story is true.

Aufgabe 3

a) Barry's Dad told him to clean up his room.
b) Barry's Dad ordered him to do his homework.
c) Barry's Dad expected him to be home by eight.
d) Barry's Dad wanted him to get a scuttle of coal for the fire.
e) Barry's Dad encouraged him to work hard at school.
f) Barry's Dad asked not to start smoking.
g) Barry's Dad advised him to become a doctor.
h) Barry's Dad begged him not to leave home.

Aufgabe 4

a) I forced myself to study hard at university.
b) ... to give me a job.
c) ... I asked Winnie to marry me.
d) I used the Rivonia Trial to attack apartheid.
e) I encouraged A.N.C. supporters to keep on fighting.
f) I warned President Botha not to let South Africa split into two hostile camps.
g) I invited President Botha to help me bring our peoples together.
h) I helped President De Klerk build a new South Africa.
i) I wrote a book to tell the story of my life.
j) I visited Germany to thank the people for their support.

Aufgabe 5

a) Eileen was the first girl to appear at the lecture / to turn up for the lecture.
b) The Inspector was the only person to come to my assistance / to my aid.
c) Don't you know how to tie a knot?
d) The Prime Minister was the last person to board the airplane.

Aufgabe 6

a) To order educational supplies you should go to O'Mahony's.
O'Mahony's is the only shop in Kerry to sell good books.
O'Mahony's is the place to buy play equipment.
b) To order a taxi you should ring John Crean at Speedy Cabs.
John Crean is the only taximan in Kerry to drive slowly.
John Crean is the man to contact if you need a taxi.
c) To test drive a new Opel Corsa you should call to Ahern's.
Ahern's is the only garage to sell the new Opel Corsa.
Ahern's is the place to meet the new Opel Corsa.
d) To buy antique furniture you should go to Lyons.
Lyons is the first place to go to for antiques.
Lyons is the place to get good bargins in antique furniture.
e) To get material printed you should go to Barry's.
Barry Print and Packaging is the last place to consider going to.
Barry Print and Packaging is the place to get calling cards printed.
f) To buy bed spreads you should go to Dan Fitzgerald's.
Fitzgerald's is the best shop to buy bed linen in.
Fitzgerald's is the place to go for linen sheets.
g) To buy a TV you should go to Culloty's.
Culloty's is the only shop in town to sell TV equipment.
Culloty's is the shop to buy a TV in.
h) To get a good pint you should go to Páidí Ó Shea's.
Páidí Ó Shea's is the best pub to hear Irish music in.
Páidí Ó Shea's is the place to go for Irish music.
i) O'Mahony's is the place where one / you can buy play equipment.
j) John Crean is the man who you should contact if you need a taxi.
k) Ahern's is the place where you can meet the new Opel Corsa.
l) Lyons is the place where one can get good bargins in antique furniture.
m) Barry Print and packaging is the place where you can get calling cards printed.
n) Fitzgerald's is the place where you should go for linen sheets.
o) Culloty's is the shop where you / one can buy a TV.
p) Páidí Ó Shea's is the place where one should go for Irish music.

Aufgabe 7

a) Why would you become a doctor?
I would become a doctor to cure the sick.

b) Why would you become a sailor?
I would become a sailor to see the world.

c) Why would you become a vet?
I would become a vet to cure sick animals.

d) Why would you become a writer?
I would become a writer to write good books.

e) Why would you become a pilot?
I would become a pilot to fly airplanes.

f) Why would you become a postman?
I would become a postman to meet people and stay fit.

g) Why would you become a newsreader?
I would become a newsreader to be on TV.

h) Why would you become a trade union official?
I would become a trade union official to fight for better pay.

Aufgabe 8

(1) tell, (2) be, (3) to forget, (4) listen, (5) drive, (6) to say, (7) work, (8) conduct, (9) to make, (10) be, (11) let, (12) roast, (13) give, (14) die, (15) to go or go, (16) die

Aufgabe 9

a) see text

b) not the first American to win, first person to follow the, knew what to do, strength to call on, was to win
Name of person: Martina Navratilova

c) Musterlösung:
To begin with let me point out that there are very few female heads of school so I expect the job is not an easy one for any woman who becomes principal. I believe that the most difficult task would be dealing with the staff because it is very important for staff to work well together. Otherwise there can be a lot of fighting and arguing and this can lead to poor morale in the school. The most important thing for students is the example they receive from teachers and it is up to the head to see that good example is shown by all staff members. Discipline is therefore vital and the female principal who has poor discipline is going to have problems. On the plus side I could imagine the job being very interesting and I think I would get great pleasure out of showing men that women can be bosses too.

8 Gerundium

Aufgabe 1

a) Getting our telephone bill is not very nice.
b) Opening the envelope and taking out the bill gives me a horrible feeling.
c) Having a telephone, a husband, two sons and two daughters is very costly!
d) Making a phonecall is difficult in my house.
e) Seeing my bank statement after my bill has been paid is unpleasant.
f) Worrying about the matter is stupid.
g) Having a chat with my neighbour, Ann Dunne, is much better.
h) Hearing the size of her telephone bill makes me feel good!

Aufgabe 2

1/G, 2/I, 3/A, 4/K, 5/H, 6/E, 7/B, 8/D, 9/J, 10/M, 11/L, 12/F, 13/C

Aufgabe 3

(1) being, (2) for, (3) helping, (4) about, (5) finding, (6) about, (7) witnessing, (8) of, (9) not being, (10) about, (11) having, (12) of, (13) watching, (14) in, (15) spreading, (16) of, (17) playing, (18) of, (19) winning

Aufgabe 4

(1) of/in, (2) playing, (3) in, (4) in/during, (5) in, (6) trying, (7) of, (8) hitting, (9) in, (10) partaking, (11) of, (12) switching, (13) to, (14) doing

Aufgabe 5

a) … crying over spilt milk.
b) … counting your chickens before they're hatched.
c) … listening to loud music.
d) … crossing the road with all the traffic nowadays.
e) … taking the money?
f) … making such noise!

Aufgabe 6

learning: gerund used as the subject of a sentence
convincing: gerund used after a particular verb + preposition
switching: gerund used because of an adjective + preposition
getting: gerund used after a definite expression
using: gerund used after noun + preposition
surprising: gerund used after a definite expression
achieving: gerund used after verb + preposition

Aufgabe 7

a) Do you remember seeing Countee Cullen in Baltimore on the day concerned?
b) Do you deny calling her a nigger?
c) Do you usually play with black children?
d) Do you get good grades at school?
e) Are you in the habit of calling people names?
f) Do you enjoy hurting people?
g) Do you admit poking out your tongue at her?
h) Are you proud of being white?
i) Do you mind blacks getting good jobs?
j) Do you dislike blacks having money?
k) Does your father employ blacks?
l) Do you know you are in danger of going to jail if found guilty?

Aufgabe 8

a) feeding, of seeing
b) saying
c) playing, working
d) talking, of hearing, to be
e) buying, run
f) Màiréad suggested boiling eggs for dinner/lunch.
g) The poor old woman continued singing/to sing even though nobody was listening.
h) Breda hates going to bed late.
i) Please avoid throwing cigarettes on the ground.
j) Harold advised her never to say that again.

Aufgabe 9

(1) of meeting, (2) of seeing, (3) to do, (4) sneaking, (5) to stay, (6) watching, (7) on having, (8) to go, (9) in talking, (10) to play, (11) to believe, (12) saying, (13) taking

Aufgabe 10

What a day I've had! Dad and I have been everywhere – all over Dublin! We started by having breakfast in the hotel. The Gresham Hotel, where we are staying, is one of Dublin's most up-market hotels. The foyer is lovely and the bedroom huge. Breakfast was as big as the dinner I normally eat! Being a guest here is a strange but nice feeling. Having finished breakfast we went for a walk to O'Connell Bridge, a nice bridge in the centre of town. The bridge is named after one of Ireland's most famous politicians Daniel O'Connell. From there we could get a great view of the River Liffey. Dad was in good form and suggested taking a tour on a bus. The bus trip took us past Trinity College, Stephen's Green and many other highlights. The best of the lot was the visit to the Guinness Brewery where we sampled the beer. Walking down Grafton Street later in the day we met some lovely people including two firemen collecting funds for some scheme or another. We had a great laugh with them and they let me take their picture. The people here strike me as very open and talkative. The worst thing about Dublin is the wind. It is unbelieveably windy here. I don't think I'd like the weather very much if I was living here. All in all though, Dublin – and Ireland in general – seems very nice. I could well imagine coming here again.

9 Partizip Präsens und Partizip Perfekt

Aufgabe 1

1 steaming: example of the participle used as adjective
2 was cascading: participle within the past continuous
3 gushing: participle the result of a particular construction (to find + water + -ing form)
4 was pouring: past continuous
5 reaching: present participle used to shorten a clause
6 draped: past participle used to shorten a relative clause
7 scalding: present participle as adjective
8 cooked: past participle used as a passive form
9 hitting: present participle instead of a subordinate clause
10 was running: present participle within past continuous
11 collapsed: past participle as part of past perfect
12 ruined: past participle used as a passive form

Aufgabe 2

(1) founded, (2) discovered, (3) built, (4) living, (5) chatting, (6) brought, (7) known, (8) leading, (9) living, (10) getting

Aufgabe 3

a) interesting
b) loving
c) surprising
d) worried
e) confused
f) annoyed
g) inspiring/inspired

Aufgabe 4

a) As a child I saw Willie Mays playing for the New York Giants.
b) Waiting for the pitcher to throw the ball, he gripped his bat tightly./ Gripping his bat tightly, he waited for the pitcher to throw the ball.
c) Crouching in anticipation, Yogi Berra, catcher of the New York Yankees, seemed sure all would go well.
d) After striking the baseball, Mays began to run./ Mays began running after he had struck the ball.
e) Hitting 660 home runs is not easy; but Willie Mays did so and thus became one of the most famous baseball players ever.
f) The baseball bat used by him can be seen today in a museum.

Aufgabe 5

(1) undertaken, (2) born, (3) known, (4) seeing, (5) building, (6) wanting, (7) writing, (8) thinking, (9) living, (10) realizing, (11) very interested

Aufgabe 6

a) His father supported a wife and six children, often working late into the night to earn more money.
b) As a child this singer dreamt of being a cowboy, practising all the usual cowboy tricks and hoping, one day, to buy a ranch and loads of livestock.
c) During his time at Oaklahoma State agricultural college he worked hard, studying late into the night to pass his exams.
d) He also loved singing, playing the guitar and composing country and western songs in his spare time.
e) As a musician he was very good, soon coming to the notice of a record company.
f) He became very famous, selling more records than any other American solo artist.
g) He has written great songs like *The Dance, You May Be Right, We Shall Be Free* always trying to speak to and for ordinary folk.
h) Thanks to his wealth he also became a cowboy, buying his family a 400 acre ranch in Nashville.

His name is Garth Brooks.

Aufgabe 7
a) This short booklet portrays/shows/outlines some of the pilot schemes/programmes already carried out.
b) The funding/financing of the RDP is the most important building stone/block of all.
c) South Africa needs/requires a culture of learning.
d) Building/The building of a culture of partnership is only beginning.

Aufgabe 8
(1) When you/one enter(s), (2) signs which show, (3) which continue, (4) after one has seen, (5) who realize, (6) which is made from, (7) which are displayed, (8) if one compares them, (9) that was killed, (10) that was felled, (11) because they believed, (12) when one leaves

10 *if*-Sätze

Aufgabe 1
a) to encourage: to stimulate someone to do something
b) a splint: a piece of material used for holding a broken bone in place
c) to refer someone: to send someone to another person e. g. to a doctor
d) a wallet: men carry money in a wallet (women use a purse)
e) ransom demand: conditions required to get a kidnapped person back
f) debt: money owed to another person
g) wireless: radio

Aufgabe 2
a) If the patient has a pain I will ask her about her diet.
If the patient had a pain I would ask her about her diet.
If the patient had had a pain I would have asked her about her diet.
b) If the patient feels very dizzy I will tell her to sit down.
If the patient felt very dizzy I would tell her to sit down.
If the patient had felt very dizzy I would have told her to sit down.
c) If the patient twists his ankle I will send him for an x-ray.
If the patient twisted his ankle I would send him for an x-ray.
If the patient had twisted his ankle I would have sent him for an x-ray.
d) If the patient suffers a broken leg I will make a splint for him.
If the patient suffered a broken leg I would make a splint for him.
If the patient had suffered a broken leg I would have made a splint for him.
e) If the patient needs an immediate operation I will call an ambulance.
If the patient needed an immediate operation I would call an ambulance.

If the patient had needed an immediate operation I would have called an ambulance.

f) If the patient smokes too much I will encourage him to stop.
If the patient smoked too much l would encourage him to stop.
If the patient had smoked too much I would have encouraged him to stop.

Aufgabe 3

a) ... would take it.
b) ... got lost she would ask a person the way.
c) ... saw a fierce dog about to attack he would run away.
d) ... cried its father would feed it.

Aufgabe 4

a) ... he would not have landed in jail.
b) ... had not asked the way she would have missed the bus. /
... the bus would have been gone.
c) ... had not run away the dog would have bitten him.
d) ... had not fed the child the baby would have kept crying.

Aufgabe 5

a) a hedge, settlers, diary, production, proof
b) will tell him, listened, don't stop, had heard, play, would have let
c) Wenn Van Riebeeck wusste, dass das Land den Eingeborenen gehörte, warum nahm er es ihnen dann weg?
Wenn Van Riebeeck wirklich Mitleid mit ihnen gehabt hätte, hätte er weit mehr für sie getan.
Wenn er freundlich mit ihnen gesprochen hätte und ihnen nie ihr Land weggenommen hätte, hätten sie ihn nicht gefragt, ob sie das gleiche in Holland tun dürften.

Aufgabe 6

a) ... will have to face the music.
To confront the result of one's actions.
b) ... she will get into hot water.
To get into trouble.
c) ... will give her the cold shoulder.
To ignore her.
d) ... will be under a cloud.
To be in shame and disgrace.

Aufgabe 7

a) should
b) would
c) would
d) should
e) would
f) would
g) should
h) should
i) would
j) would/should
k) should

Aufgabe 8

a) ... he would not have gone to Dallas.
b) ... he would not have married her.
c) ... he would not have left the hotel.
d) ... they would have sown other crops.

Aufgabe 9

a) you would not have known
b) you would not have heard of
c) would have spoken
d) would have been
e) you would have disagreed
f) you would have had to decide
g) you would have been prepared
h) you would have seen

Place: United States
Period: Civil War

Aufgabe 10

a) will have
b) will find out
c) work
d) will learn
e) will throw
f) would have
g) had not fallen
h) would have given
i) will go, is
j) would not have become
k) had not paid
l) were/was, could/would be able to

11 Relativpronomen und Relativsätze

Aufgabe 1

a) Clonmel is the name of the town in Ireland where this music session took place.
b) The woman is playing the fiddle which/that she bought years ago.
c) Who is the man whose eyes are closed?
d) The bow is a long stick which/that the fiddler is holding in her right hand.

e) These musicians, who the photographer saw in a pub, were attending the Fleadh Cheoil, an important Irish music festival.
f) The publican who asked these musicians to play was very pleased he did so.
g) The two men are playing with the fiddler who they know well.
h) Folk music is popular throughout Ireland where it is played in pubs, on street corners and at festivals.

Aufgabe 2

a) whose
b) who
c) whose
d) who's
e) who's, whose
f) whose
g) who
h) whose

Aufgabe 3

a) Ireland is a small country where poetry is very important.
b) Ireland has many literary magazines which publish both Irish and non-Irish writers.
c) Sean O'Faoláin was a famous Irish writer who published *The Bell* in the 1940s and 1950s.
d) *Innti* is a well-known publication which/that publishes poetry written in the Irish language.
e) The *Honest Ulsterman* is published in Belfast where many famous Irish poets started writing.
f) *Metre* is a Dublin magazine which often publishes translations of European poetry.
g Gerald Dawe, who is the editor of *Krino*, is also a poet.
h) *Poetry Ireland Review,* which many writers and poets submit to, is probably Ireland's best known poetry magazine.

Aufgabe 4

A/8 (which), B/6 (who), C/7 (who), D/1 (of which), E/4 (whose), F/2 (which), G/5 (which), H/3 (of which)

Aufgabe 5

a) non-defining: Willa Cather, who wrote *O Pioneers* and eleven other books not to mention 58 stories, is generally acknowledged as one of the major American fiction writers of this century.

b) defining: Louise Edrich is a writer who has a very large readership and has been translated into many languages.
c) non-defining: American works of fiction such as *In Country,* which launched Bobbie Ann Mason's career, are giving female fiction in America a good name.
d) non-defining: Alice Walker and Alison Lurie, both of whom won the Pulitzer Prize for fiction in the 1980s, are two names that come to mind when discussing important fiction in recent years.
e) defining: The short story is an important literary form which is enjoying a revival at present.
f) defining: Ann Castillo is a Hispanic writer who started publishing with small Hispanic presses in the US before moving to larger publishing houses.
g) defining: Female writers who write mainly to fight for women's rights have been loudly criticized by many male critics and writers.
h) non-defining: The imput of female American writers today, many of whom have won important prizes for their work, has been commented on by various observers.

Aufgabe 6 a) at whom
... is looking at is called Deirdre.
... that/who O'Brien is looking at is called Deirdre.
b) on which
The park bench on which they are sitting was bought by the corporation.
The park bench they are sitting on was bought by the corporation.
The park bench that/which they are sitting on was bought by the corporation.
c) to whom
The man to whom the girl is engaged works in the E.S.B.
The man the girl is engaged to works in the E.S.B.
The man that/who the girl is engaged to works in the E.S.B.
d) through which
The magazine through which she is leafing is a woman's magazine.
The magazine she is leafing through is a woman's magazine.
The magazine that/which she is leafing through is a woman's magazine.

e) about which
The things about which he is thinking change suddenly.
The things he is thinking about change suddenly.
The things that/which he is thinking about change suddenly.

f) to which
The pub to which O'Brien is going is calles O'Reilly's.
The pub O'Brien is going to is called O'Reilly's.
The pub which/that O'Brien is going to is called O'Reilly's.

Aufgabe 7 (1) who, (2) whose, (3) which/that, (4) who, (5) which/that, (6) whose, (7) who/whom, (8) which, (9) where, (10) which/that, (11) who, (12) whose, (13) who, (14) whom, (15) whose, (16) who, (17) what, (18) that

Aufgabe 8
a) ... who is speaking to the Prime Minister ...
The man speaking to the Prime Minster works in Downing Street.
b) ... which/that the man is carrying is heavy.
The box the man is carrying is heavy.
c) ... who /that is playing with the children is the Prime Minister's wife.
The woman playing with the children is the Prime Minister's wife.
d) ... which/that are hanging in the room are nice.
The curtains hanging in the room are nice.
e) ... which/that is hanging on the wall is also nice.
The picture hanging on the wall is also nice.
f) ... who/that are playing with their mother are young.
The children playing with their mother are young.
g) ... which/that is standing in the room is old.
The table standing in the room is old.
h) for the student to decide
i) for the student to decide

Aufgabe 9 The village I live in, Dunmore East, is on the south coast of Ireland. The nearest city is at least ten miles away though we get a lot of visitors who drive out from there in the summer. Dunmore is a fishing village and though my Dad's a teacher he often takes me fishing in our small boat. I love the sea and would hate it if we lived in a city or midland town. If the weather is good we play on the beach but best of all I like to go walking along the cliffs when a wild storm is raging. If the weather is bad all the local boats take shelter in the harbour. My sister Mary loves birds and if ever they fly into our yard she goes out feeding them as fast as she can. If seagulls come round I chase them away as they can be awful loud at times. I wouldn't live in a city if you gave me all the money in the world. If ever you would like to visit our village be sure and do so – it's worth the trip.

12 Indirekte Rede

Aufgabe 1

a) ... (that) that Model T Ford was his favourite vintage car.
b) ... that he had taken it out for a short spin the week before that.
c) ... said that their grandfather had bought the car a long time before that.
d) ... told Enda that they had better jump in then because it was time to go.
e) ... remarked that those old cars were fantastic.
f) ... said that was the lucky charm his grandfather had always worn when driving.
g) ... said that he had checked the brakes the day before.
h) ... said (that) that was great fun.
i) ... said that as kids they had loved cleaning that car.
j) ... told him that his grandfather had taken good care of that car.
k) ... said he would start then and told her to hold on to her hat.
l) ... said they would be in Navan before long.

Aufgabe 2

a) The D. J. said that *When I'm Sixty-Four* had been a very early Paul McCartney composition.
b) ... that the sound effects on *Lovely Rita* had been created by using combs and toilet paper and that once The Beatles had recorded the sounds they had played them backwards and had liked what they had heard!
c) ... that Actress Mae West had at first refused to allow her image to appear on the album cover but that she had gone back on her intial decision after the Beatles had written to her.
d) ... that *A Day in the Life* had been banned by the B.B.C.
e) ... that Spiro Agnew, the well-known American politician, had led a crusade to ban *With a Little Help from My Friends.*
f) ... a TV commercial for Kellogs' Cornflakes had inspired John Lennon to write *Good Morning, Good Morning.*

g) … that John Lennon had found the lyrics for *Being for the Benefit of Mr Kite* on a antique poster which had been used in 1843 to advertize a circus in Rochdale.
h) … it hadn't taken the album long to sell more than ten million copies worldwide and that must be a record!
i) … that the man who had blown his mind out in *A Day in the Life* had been Tars Browne, heir to the Guinness fortune.

Aufgabe 3
a) … that the guardian spirit of Irish poetry had like his predecessor, Yeats, received his just recognition.
b) … that that day's announcement was especially exciting because Seamus was in the middle of his best work.
c) … that she had felt very emotional, tears had come and it had been a mixture of joy and sadness, for the old times.
d) … that the last time he had seen him, four months before that, he had charmed a 2,000 strong audience of A/Level students.
e) … that at first he had thought he must be dreaming (but) then he was thrilled to be there representing the Irish Government at that time.
f) … much would be made of the fact that the prize had gone to a Northern poet who had chosen to make his home in the South; and no doubt there would be mutterings from many quarters that the Nobel committee had once again made a political choice by awarding the prize to an Irishman at the end of a year which had been one of the most hopeful yet perilously balanced periods in the history of their two states."
g) … he had to buy his book *The Spirit Level* the following day.

Aufgabe 4
George Washinton told the audience (that) his great-grandfather had emigrated from England in protest after King George I had been defeated by Cromwell. His family had been living there in Virginia for many years. He said that they owned a lot of land along the Potomac. Mathematics had been his favourite subject at school. His father had died when he had been a teenager so he had come to look on his brother Lawrence as his closest relative. Unfortunately, he too had passed away some years before that. He related how, at the age of 19, he had become a wealthy landowner. In 1753, he had been commissioned to visit and deliver a letter to the French forces on the Ohio. That must have been his first test as a military leader he said. A long time before that all he had wanted was to acquire land but that trip had stirred a real sense of patriotism

in him. And he said he would tell us something else; he might never have become a general had it not been for his wife! She had given him wonderful support all his life and he had loved her two children as if they had been his own. He maintained he would be very surprised if the colonies didn't become independent in the course of his lifetime. He only hoped they would do so without bloodshed.

Aufgabe 5

a) He asked if I had got on well with my father.
b) She enquired if my family had always lived in Virginia.
c) One man asked if my mother was still alive.
d) A little boy wanted to know how my brother had died.
e) He also asked how long I had known my wife.
f) A girl asked me what I thought of the British Stamp Act.
g) She also asked if it was hard to be a British subject living in Virginia.
h) I was asked if I was friends with General Forbes.
i) One man asked me if I intended to go back to farming.
j) He then enquired if the colonies would ever become independent.
k) A woman asked me if I would be prepared to fight the British.
l) Then she wanted to know if I would dine with them tonight.
m) Someone asked me when I would see my family again.
n) I was asked if I read much.
o) The same person wanted to know who my favourite writer was.

Aufgabe 6

a) Peary advised the others to push on with all possible speed.
b) Peary told them not to let him sleep for longer than 4 hours.
c) He ordered them to overhaul and strengthen the sledges.
d) He said they should set their course by the moon.
e) He said not to camp there.
f) He instructed them to cross the lead.
g) He gave orders to overtake them and give them fuel.
h) He announced they/he had to cover 30 miles the following day.
i) He said never to travel without women.
j) He told them to turn in and sleep.
k) He said to be sure and rest the dogs.
l) He said not to worry too much.
m) He told them to tell him when the sun was up.
n) His wife said he had to come home.

Aufgabe 7

a) The presenter announced that a series of bomb hoaxes had thrown the London underground into chaos that morning. Across the city people on their way to work had been left stranded as police had cleared eight railway stations in the capital. The loss to the economy in earnings and production would not be known until later that week but it was estimated to run into millions of pounds. The announcer said that police had been asking for help with the investigation and that afternoon a hotline number had been set up. He asked if we could help? He mentioned that a police constable was waiting 24 hours a day to take our calls. He said we just might have seen or heard something that would lead to an arrest. The number to ring was 0171–565677.

b) The first Londoner asked who did that sort of thing? Was it a crackpot or was that 9/11 all over again. He said whoever it was they must be sick. He said he had been on his way to work when it had happened. He said he had ended up four hours late.

c) A Second Londoner said he couldn't understand those people.

d) A Third Londoner asked if that was for real? He said the year before a friend of his had been killed by a bomb. He continued by saying that those lunatics just didn't give a hoot.

Aufgabe 8

The President began by saying there had been a change of government. It had begun two years before that, when the House of Representatives had become Democratic by a decisive majority. It had now been completed. The President continued by saying that the Senate about to assemble would also be democratic. The offices of President and Vice-President had been put into the hands of Democrats. The President asked what that meant? That, he said was the question that was uppermost in (our) minds on that day. That is the question he was going to try and answer, in order, if he might, to interpret the occasion. It meant he said much more than the mere success of a party. The success of a party meant little except when the Nation was using that party for large and definite purpose. He said no one could mistake the purpose for which the nation now sought to use the Democratic Party. It sought to use it to interpret a change in its own plans and point of view. Some old things with which we had grown familiar, and which had begun to creep into the very habit of our thought and our lives, had altered their aspect as we had latterly looked critically upon them, with fresh, awakened eyes …

Aufgabe 9

a) might
b) could
c) had to
d) must
e) could
f) might
g) that day
h) the day before that
i) the week before last
j) then
k) there
l) that
m) those
n) his/her
o) their
p) the year before that
q) two weeks before (that)
r) he/she would go
s) he/she was going

13 Schwierige Aufgaben zum Knobeln

Aufgabe 1

a) When he was a child John wanted to become a teacher.
b) May I see the Menu please.
c) My boss worked as a chef/cook in a hotel for 3 years.
d) In his view/opinion he is the best teacher in the school.
e) The High School/Secondary School has a good name/reputation.
f) We've got a new English teacher.
g) What does this question mean?
h) Children have a wonderful imagination.
i) The company/firm was founded in 1987.
j) Could you make a cup of tea for me?
k) My hair is much too long.
l) This jam tastes great.
m) The bus driver checked/controlled our bus tickets.
n) Please check/examine his papers/identity card.
o) The doctor wrote a prescription.
p) Yesterday evening the BBC broadcast a very good programme on Russia.
q) Can you give me your recipe for Irish coffee?
r) Did you get tickets for the game?
s) My office has to be cleaned every week.

Aufgabe 2

a) met
b) has broken
c) shattered
d) Did you lock
e) Have you got
f) shrank

g) cut
h) set
i) lay
j) wove

Aufgabe 3 Check pages 168–171

Aufgabe 4
a) London
b) Paris
c) Washington
d) Toronto
e) Moscow
f) Glasgow
g) Perth

Aufgbe 5
a) S
b) gone
c) M
d) love
e) Starr
f) visa
g) money
h) e
i) SOS

word: SOMETIMES

Aufgabe 6
a) footpath/pavement (noun)
b) showroom (noun)
c) across (preposition)
d) gets (verb)
e) pavement/footpath (noun)
f) for (preposition)
g) the (definite article)
h) owner (noun)
i) lazy (adjective)
j) by (preposition)
k) on (preposition)
l) angry (adjective)
m) in (preposition)
n) traffic warden (noun)

Ihre Meinung ist uns wichtig!

Ihre Anregungen sind uns immer willkommen. Bitte informieren Sie uns mit diesem Schein über Ihre Verbesserungsvorschläge!

Titel-Nr.	Seite	Vorschlag

Bitte hier abtrennen

16-V1M

Bitte ausfüllen und im frankierten Umschlag
an uns einsenden. Für Fensterkuverts geeignet.

Zutreffendes bitte ankreuzen!

Die Absenderin/der Absender ist:

- ☐ Lehrer/in in den Klassenstufen: ____
- ☐ Fachbetreuer/in
  Fächer: ____
- ☐ Seminarlehrer/in
  Fächer: ____
- ☐ Regierungsfachberater/in
  Fächer: ____
- ☐ Oberstufenbetreuer/in
- ☐ Schulleiter/in
- ☐ Referendar/in, Termin 2. Staatsexamen: ____
- ☐ Leiter/in Lehrerbibliothek
- ☐ Leiter/in Schülerbibliothek
- ☐ Sekretariat
- ☐ Eltern
- ☐ Schüler/in, Klasse: ____
- ☐ Sonstiges: ____

Unterrichtsfächer: (Bei Lehrkräften!)

____

STARK Verlag
Postfach 1852
85318 Freising

Kennen Sie Ihre Kundennummer?
Bitte hier eintragen.

Absender (Bitte in Druckbuchstaben!)

Name/Vorname

Straße/Nr.

PLZ/Ort

Telefon privat **Geburtsjahr**

E-Mail-Adresse

Schule/Schulstempel (Bitte immer angeben!)

Bitte hier abtrennen

Sicher durch alle Klassen!

Lernerfolg durch selbstständiges Üben zu Hause! Die von Fachlehrern entwickelten Trainingsbände enthalten alle nötigen Fakten und jede Menge praxiserprobte Übungen mit schülergerechten Lösungen.

Mathematik: Training

Übertritt in weiterführende Schulen 4. Klasse .... Best.-Nr. 990404
Mathematik – Übertritt ins Gymnasium .... Best.-Nr. 90002
Mathematik 5. Klasse Bayern .... Best.-Nr. 90005
Mathematik 5. Klasse Baden-Württemberg .... Best.-Nr. 80005
Mathematik 5. Klasse .... Best.-Nr. 900051
Mathematik 6. Klasse Bayern .... Best.-Nr. 900062
Mathematik 6. Klasse .... Best.-Nr. 90006
Bruchzahlen und Dezimalbrüche .... Best.-Nr. 900061
Algebra 7. Klasse .... Best.-Nr. 900111
Geometrie 7. Klasse .... Best.-Nr. 90021
Algebra 8. Klasse .... Best.-Nr. 90012
Geometrie 8. Klasse .... Best.-Nr. 90022
Lineare Gleichungssysteme .... Best.-Nr. 900122
Algebra 9. Klasse .... Best.-Nr. 90013
Geometrie 9. Klasse .... Best.-Nr. 90023
Klassenarbeiten Mathematik 9. Klasse .... Best.-Nr. 900331
Satzgruppe des Pythagoras .... Best.-Nr. 900232
Algebra 10. Klasse .... Best.-Nr. 90014
Geometrie 10. Klasse .... Best.-Nr. 90024
Potenzen und Potenzfunktionen .... Best.-Nr. 900141
Klassenarbeiten Mathematik 10. Klasse .... Best.-Nr. 900341
Wiederholung Algebra .... Best.-Nr. 90009
Kompakt-Wissen Algebra .... Best.-Nr. 90016
Kompakt-Wissen Geometrie .... Best.-Nr. 90026

Mathematik: Zentrale Prüfungen

Bayerischer Mathematik-Test (BMT)
8. Klasse Gymnasium Bayern .... Best.-Nr. 950081
Bayerischer Mathematik-Test (BMT)
10. Klasse Gymnasium Bayern .... Best.-Nr. 950001
Vergleichsarbeiten Mathematik
6. Klasse Gymnasium Baden-Württemberg .... Best.-Nr. 850061
Vergleichsarbeiten Mathematik
8. Klasse Gymnasium Baden-Württemberg .... Best.-Nr. 850081
Zentrale Klassenarbeit Mathematik
10. Klasse Gymnasium Baden-Württemberg .... Best.-Nr. 80001
Zentrale Prüfung Mathematik Klasse 10
Gymnasium Nordrhein-Westfalen .... Best.-Nr. 550001
Zentrale Prüfung Mathematik Jahrgangsstufe 10
Gymnasium Brandenburg .... Best.-Nr. 1250001
Zentrale Prüfung Mathematik Jahrgangsstufe 10
Gymnasium Mecklenburg-Vorpommern .... Best.-Nr. 1350001
Besondere Leistungsfeststellung Mathematik
10. Klasse Gymnasium Sachsen .... Best.-Nr. 1450001
Besondere Leistungsfeststellung Mathematik
10. Klasse Gymnasium Thüringen .... Best.-Nr. 165001

Physik

Physik – Mittelstufe 1 .... Best.-Nr. 90301
Physik – Mittelstufe 2 .... Best.-Nr. 90302

Deutsch: Training

Übertritt in weiterführende Schulen mit CD .... Best.-Nr. 994402
Rechtschreibung und Diktat 5./6. Klasse .... Best.-Nr. 90408
Nach den neuen Regeln, gültig ab 01.08.06.
Grammatik und Stil 5./6. Klasse
Bayern, Baden-Württemberg .... Best.-Nr. 90406
Grammatik und Stil 5./6. Klasse .... Best.-Nr. 50406
Aufsatz 5./6. Klasse .... Best.-Nr. 90401
Grammatik und Stil 7./8. Klasse .... Best.-Nr. 90407
Aufsatz 7./8. Klasse .... Best.-Nr. 90403
Aufsatz 9./10. Klasse .... Best.-Nr. 90404
Deutsche Rechtschreibung 5.–10. Klasse .... Best.-Nr. 90402
Nach den neuen Regeln, gültig ab 01.08.06.
Übertritt in die Oberstufe .... Best.-Nr. 90409
Kompakt-Wissen Rechtschreibung .... Best.-Nr. 944065
Nach den neuen Regeln, gültig ab 01.08.06.
Lexikon zur Kinder- und Jugendliteratur .... Best.-Nr. 93443

Deutsch: Zentrale Prüfungen

Jahrgangsstufentest Deutsch
6. Klasse Gymnasium Bayern .... Best.-Nr. 954061
Jahrgangsstufentest Deutsch
8. Klasse Gymnasium Bayern .... Best.-Nr. 954081
Zentrale Klassenarbeit Deutsch
10. Klasse Gymnasium Baden-Württemberg .... Best.-Nr. 80402
Zentrale Prüfung Deutsch Klasse 10
Gymnasium Nordrhein-Westfalen .... Best.-Nr. 554001
Zentrale Prüfung Deutsch Jahrgangsstufe 10
Gymnasium Brandenburg .... Best.-Nr. 1254001
Zentrale Prüfung Deutsch Jahrgangsstufe 10
Gymnasium Mecklenburg-Vorpommern .... Best.-Nr. 1354001
Besondere Leistungsfeststellung Deutsch
10. Klasse Gymnasium Sachsen .... Best.-Nr. 1454001
Besondere Leistungsfeststellung Deutsch
10. Klasse Gymnasium Thüringen .... Best.-Nr. 165401

(Bitte blättern Sie um)

Englisch Grundwissen

Englisch Grundwissen 5. Klasse
Bayern, Baden-Württemberg .... Best.-Nr. 90505
Englisch Grundwissen 5. Klasse .... Best.-Nr. 50505
Klassenarbeiten Englisch 5. Klasse mit CD .... Best.-Nr. 905053
Englisch Grundwissen 6. Klasse
Bayern, Baden-Württemberg .... Best.-Nr. 90506
Englisch Grundwissen 6. Klasse .... Best.-Nr. 50506
Klassenarbeiten Englisch 6. Klasse mit CD .... Best.-Nr. 905063
Englisch Grundwissen
1. Lernjahr als 2. Fremdsprache
Bayern, Baden-Württemberg .... Best.-Nr. 905052
Englisch Grundwissen
1. Lernjahr als 2. Fremdsprache .... Best.-Nr. 505052
Englisch Grundwissen
2. Lernjahr als 2. Fremdsprache
Bayern, Baden-Württemberg .... Best.-Nr. 905062
Englisch Grundwissen
2. Lernjahr als 2. Fremdsprache .... Best.-Nr. 505062
Englisch Grundwissen 7. Klasse .... Best.-Nr. 90507
Englisch Grundwissen 8. Klasse .... Best.-Nr. 90508
Englisch Grundwissen 9. Klasse .... Best.-Nr. 90509
Englisch Grundwissen 10. Klasse .... Best.-Nr. 90510
Englisch Übertritt in die Oberstufe .... Best.-Nr. 82453
Kompakt-Wissen Kurzgrammatik .... Best.-Nr. 90461

Englisch Textproduktion

Textproduktion 9./10. Klasse .... Best.-Nr. 90541

Englisch Leseverstehen

Leseverstehen 5. Klasse .... Best.-Nr. 90526
Leseverstehen 6. Klasse .... Best.-Nr. 90525
Leseverstehen 8. Klasse .... Best.-Nr. 90522
Leseverstehen 10. Klasse .... Best.-Nr. 90521

Englisch Hörverstehen

Hörverstehen 5. Klasse mit CD .... Best.-Nr. 90512
Hörverstehen 6. Klasse mit CD .... Best.-Nr. 90511
Hörverstehen 7. Klasse mit CD .... Best.-Nr. 90513
Hörverstehen 9. Klasse mit CD .... Best.-Nr. 90515
Hörverstehen 10. Klasse mit CD .... Best.-Nr. 80457

Englisch Rechtschreibung

Rechtschreibung und Diktat
5. Klasse mit 3 CDs .... Best.-Nr. 90531
Rechtschreibung und Diktat
6. Klasse mit CD .... Best.-Nr. 90532
Englische Rechtschreibung 9./10. Klasse .... Best.-Nr. 80453

Englisch Wortschatzübung

Wortschatzübung 5. Klasse mit CD .... Best.-Nr. 90518
Wortschatzübung 6. Klasse mit CD .... Best.-Nr. 90519
Wortschatzübung Mittelstufe .... Best.-Nr. 90520

Englisch Übersetzung

Translation Practice 1 / ab 9. Klasse .... Best.-Nr. 80451
Translation Practice 2 / ab 10. Klasse .... Best.-Nr. 80452

Englisch: Zentrale Prüfungen

Jahrgangsstufentest Englisch
6. Klasse mit CD Gymnasium Bayern .... Best.-Nr. 954661
Zentrale Klassenarbeit Englisch mit CD
10. Klasse Gymnasium Baden-Württemberg .... Best.-Nr. 80456
Mittlerer Schulabschluss/Sek I
Mündliche Prüfung Englisch Brandenburg .... Best.-Nr. 121550
Besondere Leistungsfeststellung Englisch mit CD
10. Klasse Gymnasium Sachsen .... Best.-Nr. 1454601
Besondere Leistungsfeststellung Englisch
10. Klasse Gymnasium Thüringen .... Best.-Nr. 165461

Französisch

Rechtschreibung und Diktat 1./2. Lernjahr
mit 2 CDs .... Best.-Nr. 905501
Französisch im 2. Lernjahr .... Best.-Nr. 905503
Französisch im 3. Lernjahr .... Best.-Nr. 905504
Wortschatzübung Mittelstufe .... Best.-Nr. 94510
Kompakt-Wissen Kurzgrammatik .... Best.-Nr. 945011
Zentrale Klassenarbeit Französisch
10. Klasse Gymnasium Baden-Württemberg .... Best.-Nr. 80501

Latein

Latein I/II im 1. Lernjahr 5./6. Klasse G8 .... Best.-Nr. 906051
Latein I/II im 2. Lernjahr 6./7. Klasse G8 .... Best.-Nr. 906061
Latein I/II im 1. Lernjahr 5./7. Klasse G9 .... Best.-Nr. 90605
Latein I – 6. Kl. Latein als 1. Fremdsprache G9 .... Best.-Nr. 90606
Latein II im 2. Lernjahr .... Best.-Nr. 906082
Übersetzung im 1. Lektürejahr G9 .... Best.-Nr. 906091
Wiederholung Grammatik .... Best.-Nr. 94601
Wortkunde .... Best.-Nr. 94603
Kompakt-Wissen Kurzgrammatik .... Best.-Nr. 906011

Biologie/Chemie

Besondere Leistungsfeststellung Biologie
10. Klasse Gymnasium Thüringen .... Best.-Nr. 165701
Besondere Leistungsfeststellung Chemie
10. Klasse Gymnasium Thüringen .... Best.-Nr. 165731
Chemie 8. Klasse Bayern .... Best.-Nr. 90731
Chemie – Mittelstufe 1 .... Best.-Nr. 80731

Geschichte

Kompakt-Wissen Geschichte
Unter-/Mittelstufe .... Best.-Nr. 907601

Ratgeber „Richtig Lernen"

Tipps und Lernstrategien – Unterstufe .... Best.-Nr. 10481
Tipps und Lernstrategien – Mittelstufe .... Best.-Nr. 10482